THE
LITTLE
BOOK
OF
MANCHESTER

STUART HYLTON

The History Press

Front cover photography: SAKhanPhotography via iStock.

First published 2013
Reprinted 2015
This edition published 2023

The History Press
97 St George's Place, Cheltenham,
Gloucestershire, GL50 3QB
www.thehistorypress.co.uk

British Library Cataloguing in Publication Data.
A catalogue record for this book is available from the British Library.

ISBN 978 1 80399 428 4

Typesetting and origination by The History Press
Printed and bound in Great Britain by TJ Books Limited, Padstow, Cornwall.

Trees for LYfe

CONTENTS

INTRODUCTION

Ever since I came to Manchester in the 1960s to study, and then stayed on to work, the city has held a special place in my affections. It was where my interest in local history really began (despite my having grown up in Windsor, which, one might have thought, had a fair amount of its own local history on offer). I later wrote a history of the city, now in its second edition, but I appreciate that not everyone wants, or has the time, to read a continuous narrative running to almost 300 pages.

This little book draws upon that longer work, but makes no pretence to be a comprehensive history of Manchester. Rather, it groups snippets from the city's past by topic and tries to present them in a way that enables the reader to dip in and out of them, as their interest and opportunity dictates.

Manchester has a long and fascinating history. Its first recorded settlement was in the same year that the eruption of Vesuvius destroyed the Roman city of Pompeii, and for the past 260 years at least, it has been at the forefront of so much of our development as a nation. I have tried to highlight some of the contributions that Manchester has given to Britain and the world. It is a vibrant and constantly changing city but it has also retained many important reminders of its past glory. I have singled out some of these, but no doubt you will have your own views on which buildings best tell its story. There is also a darker side to Manchester's development, and there can be few cities where the human cost of the Industrial Revolution has been better documented. I hope I have also given adequate recognition to this aspect of our history.

One important question is 'what is Manchester?' Its boundaries have been constantly spreading since it was first incorporated as a borough in 1838. Before that, the medieval parish boundaries stretched in many directions, far beyond even those of the present city. I must confess to having played fast and loose with those boundaries, referring to events in areas which took place before those areas became part of the modern city. I have even, on occasion, looked at events in areas which are not, and never have been, within the city's limits, where these seemed important to life in Manchester. Let us say that I have been more interested in Manchester's zone of influence, rather than its strict administrative boundaries.

Most of all, I hope this little book will stimulate your interest in the story of Manchester and encourage you to find out more. Manchester is fortunate in the many good books that have been published about its past. A visit to your local library or (better still!) bookseller is highly recommended, and there is always that internet thing!

Stuart Hylton, 2023

1

MADE IN MANCHESTER

Over the centuries, Manchester has often led the nation, and in some cases the world, in innovation. Here, we look at a few important examples. In addition, we will look at a few of the brand names that Manchester gave the nation. In particular, Manchester has led the way with innovations in transport, as the following examples show.

THE DUKE'S CUT

Before the canal age proper, a number of schemes were carried out to improve the natural corridors of transport provided by rivers. These included the Mersey and Irwell Navigation, which was approved by parliament in 1721 to make the Mersey and its tributary, the Irwell, navigable between Liverpool and Manchester. The works involved included the construction of eight locks along the route, but essentially followed the twists and turns of the rivers. The company had an effective monopoly, which allowed them to be over-priced and inefficient. They did not even use horses to pull the barges, but relied purely on manpower.

At this time, the only way of getting coal from the Duke of Bridgewater's mines at Worsley to Manchester was in 140lb bags carried by packhorses, which meant that the price of coal doubled between the pithead and Manchester. In 1736, a revolutionary proposal to construct the nation's first completely artificial waterway was given parliamentary approval. Its sponsor was the Duke of Bridgewater himself, who had been inspired by seeing the French Canal du Midi while on the grand tour. As part of the scheme, he undertook to deliver coal into Manchester for no more than 4*d* a hundredweight.

Having obtained further parliamentary approval for revisions to the scheme in 1759, Bridgewater appointed as his chief engineer the son of a crofter, a man who was unqualified and virtually illiterate. He worked without the aid of technical drawings or written instructions and had never built a canal before; when asked to explain the principles of his Barton Aqueduct to a parliamentary committee, he carved a model of it out of cheese. In every other respect, James Brindley turned out to be an inspired choice. He worked closely on the project with Bridgewater's agent John Gilbert, who is probably owed a good deal of credit for the success of the scheme, which opened for business in 1761. Soon, coal was being offloaded in Manchester at a rate of five tons an hour.

The Barton Aqueduct was the crowning glory of the scheme, though much of the public opinion thought such a feat of engineering insanely ambitious. At 200 yards long, it carried the waterway over the River Irwell at a height of 38ft, into Manchester. At the Worsley end, the canal went right into the mine itself and, by 1776, the Duke had secured a further western extension, via the Trent and Mersey Canal, to the Mersey itself, putting the Bridgewater in direct competition with the Mersey and Irwell Navigation.

The Canal even became an early tourist attraction. From 1766, people were making the trip from Manchester to explore the mines. The philosopher Jean-Jacques Rousseau and the King of Denmark were among the early tourists making the trip. Passenger services between Manchester and Liverpool were also introduced from 1776. A traveller in 1785 reported that these had two classes of accommodation and (curiously) that, in the event of 'improper conduct' by passengers, the master of the barge had the power to leave the miscreants on the bank.

But building the canal did not come cheap; the overall cost at the time was £220,000 and, by the time it was completed, the Duke was the modern-day equivalent of £2 million in debt. However, the canal was a commercial success from the start and became the inspiration for the period of canal mania that was to seize the country in the 1790s. Their golden age would cease from the 1830s onwards, as the railway network began to spread across the land.

THE BIG DITCH

If the Bridgewater was Britain's first true canal, the Manchester Ship Canal (known to locals as the 'Big Ditch') was one of its last and most ambitious. The cost and delay involved in moving goods between Manchester and the port of Liverpool has been a bone of contention at various times in both cities' histories. Ideas of linking Manchester directly to the sea go back as far as 1824, but it was not until 1882 that a detailed, thought-through and costed scheme was published. A three-year battle followed to get the scheme approved by parliament, and Manchester celebrated with parades and a public holiday when this was achieved in August 1885. Raising the necessary finance was the next headache and only two-thirds of the money needed had been assembled by the time the first ceremonial turf was cut at Eastham in November 1887.

Nonetheless, work proceeded, with as many as 16,000 people employed in the enterprise. By 1890 it became clear that the scheme was seriously under-capitalised. It was originally budgeted in 1882 at £4.5 million, but would eventually come in at around £15 million – £2 million of this would come from Manchester City Council, who became the majority interest on the board.

The project was a massive undertaking, digging a canal 35.5 miles long, 28ft deep by 170ft wide, and involved removing some 53.5 million cubic yards of material. Right up until the

Second World War, there were only six ships in existence too big to use it. Five railway lines had to be lifted over it, at a height of 75ft, and the tidal River Gowy carried underneath it in a giant iron siphon. Brindley's Barton Aqueduct, part of the Bridgewater Canal and, in its day, one of the engineering wonders of the world, had to be demolished and replaced by the Barton Swing Aqueduct. This was itself a wonder, involving a rotating trough of water 18ft wide, 6ft deep and 234ft long, able to carry barges across the Ship Canal.

The canal opened to traffic at the very start of 1894, prior to its formal opening by Queen Victoria the following May. After a slow start, the tonnage passing through it began to increase steadily, from 1.8 million in 1896 to 16.25 million in 1972. As early as 1914, the Ship Canal carried 5 per cent of Britain's imports and 4 per cent of her exports. But after the Second World War, danger signs became increasingly apparent. Larger ships, too big to use the canal, were coming into wider use; more freight was being containerised, and Manchester had no suitable site for a container port; cheap and speedy road freight eroded the commercial advantage of direct access to Manchester, as did the extra day required to navigate the canal at a time when shipping companies looked for ever faster turnaround of their fleets. Air freight also emerged as a new form of competition. By the 1980s, the original raison d'etre for the canal had gone, and it is retained today primarily for leisure use and as part of the waterways network serving Manchester (without which, parts of the city would be more prone to flooding).

THE FIRST BUS SERVICE

In 1824 a Pendleton tollkeeper, John Greenwood, set up Britain's first true public bus service and probably one of the first in the world. It ran from Market Street in the centre of Manchester and served some of the town's new suburbs – Pendleton, Ardwick and Cheetham Hill. The fare was 6*d* inside and 4*d* outside and the first vehicles could carry just eleven

people and ran three times a day. Passengers could be picked up or dropped off at any point along the route. Greenwood's was the first of many similar initiatives – by 1850, sixty-four services were operating. A man named MacEwan further developed the service by introducing far larger vehicles, drawn by three horses and able to carry seventeen inside and twenty-five outside. With these, he was able to offer a service between Strangeways and All Saints for just 3*d*, half the price of his rivals.

By 1865, most of the main routes into Manchester were served by buses, operated by a variety of carriers. The first tramway in the area made its appearance in 1862, linking Manchester and Salford – the initiative of a Manchester councillor, John Howarth. This was before the General Tramways Act of 1870 gave local authorities powers to construct and own (but not run) tramways. Manchester Corporation resisted several piecemeal attempts by private operators to set up tramways, on the grounds that it should be a municipal undertaking. By 1875 they had obtained the necessary powers to do so and within two years were in a position to start letting leases to those who would operate them. Everyone did well out of them – the operators turned a healthy profit; the council saw its development costs recouped within seventeen years and the rates subsidised to the tune of £97,600, and the passengers got regulated fares, including cheap workmen's cars during the rush hours.

It was Glasgow, not Manchester, that was the first to be a municipal operator of the tramcar service, but Manchester followed closely in their wake. By 1897 they had acquired the power not just to run the trams but also to convert them to electric traction. Gradually, the private operators' leases fell in and, by 1903, all 56 miles of the city's tramways were in municipal ownership. Municipal operation and electrification together had a dramatic effect on the operation. By 1909, fares were reduced by 40 per cent, the annual subsidy to the rates was increased ten-fold and even the working hours for the staff were reduced, from seventy to fifty-four, and their wages increased. The council diversified into petrol buses (in an effort to protect the trams from competition) and even introduced long-distance express services and a parcel delivery service. The latter turned out to be illegal and had to be largely discontinued.

At its peak, Manchester had the most extensive tramway network in the country, outside London, with (as at 1929) a fleet of 953 trams. One problem with the trams, as the city's traffic grew, was that they were rather dangerous for passengers boarding and leaving them. They tended to stop in the middle of the road, leaving passengers to fight their way through the other traffic to or from the pavement as best they could. The City Coroner reported seventy deaths and 1,147 serious injuries from this in 1921 alone. After much debate, trams started to be phased out in favour of motorbuses from 1929. A timetable to phase out the last trams by February 1939 was put on ice, as people came to realise the difficulty of ensuring the necessary supplies of petrol for the buses in a possible future wartime, and it was not until January 1949 that the last tram ran on Manchester's streets. Today, just one relic of Manchester's old tramways exists – a short section operated by volunteer enthusiasts in Heaton Park but, since 1992, a new generation of trams have appeared on the city's streets.

THE MODERN RAILWAY

While other railway lines (notably that from Stockton to Darlington) can lay claim to greater antiquity, the Liverpool to Manchester line was the first to be recognisably like its modern counterpart – twin-tracked, with recognisable stations (or stopping points), not allowing the chaos of universal access to the tracks, steam locomotive-hauled throughout and operating to a timetable (of sorts).

The original reason for its existence was the slowness, cost and unreliability of the canals that bought raw cotton and other imports to Manchester from the Liverpool docks and carried finished textiles in the other direction. Passengers were very much an afterthought in the promoters' plans. George Stephenson was appointed as engineer to the project in 1824, prior to the completion of his Stockton to Darlington line. He faced widespread opposition (and sometimes outright violence) from landowners and others when he tried to survey the route, some of which had to be done in secret by night. This, and his lack of education, may help to account for serious errors in his proposals, which were ruthlessly exploited by the opposition when it went before parliament.

When the scheme was thrown out, Stephenson was relieved of his duties and the more experienced (at least, in everything but railway building) team of George and John Rennie was bought in. Their skills (not least in negotiation) won over some key opponents to the scheme, in particular the Marquis of Stafford, heir to the Duke of Bridgewater and his canal. The scheme received parliamentary approval at the second attempt and Stephenson, his reputation somewhat restored by the successful opening of the Stockton to Darlington railway, was re-engaged to build it. Overcoming great difficulties on the way (not least, crossing the seemingly bottomless swamp of Chat Moss) the line was completed by 1830. One further problem had been securing a terminus anywhere near the centre of Manchester, again due to landowner opposition. Liverpool Road station was at that time virtually on the edge of open countryside.

Meanwhile, the promoters needed to make their minds up about how traffic would move along the line. Steam locomotives were far from being proven at this time, and there was significant support for the idea of wagons cable-hauled by stationary steam engines, at least on parts of the route. It was decided in 1829 to hold trials at Rainhill, offering a £500 prize for the 'most improved' locomotive. A shortlist of entrants was selected from a wide selection of more or less eccentric proposals, and the winner of the trials became just about the most famous locomotive in railway history – Stephenson's *Rocket*.

The official opening of the line was set for 15 September 1830. Among the dignitaries attending was the Prime Minister, the Duke of Wellington (despite him disapproving of railways, on the grounds that 'they encourage the lower classes to travel about'). Huge crowds gathered at either end of the line to witness the opening, which was marred by a fatal accident to local MP and former President of the Board of Trade William Huskisson. He dismounted from the train (against instructions) during a water stop to converse with the Prime Minister, and was run over by a locomotive.

The great surprise, once the line was opened, was a huge and unanticipated boom in passenger traffic, so great that there was no spare capacity for the railway to carry the freight for which it was originally built – more locomotives had to be ordered first. It fell to Liverpool and Manchester to work out from scratch the operating rules for a modern railway, the like of which the world had not previously seen.

THE SUBMARINE

If asked to name the person who invented the modern submarine, the curate of a church in Moss Side might not be the first person who springs to mind, but the Revd George Garrett (1852–1902) has a very good claim to that title. Strangely enough, the church seems to have a long-standing fascination with underwater travel – as long ago as 1634 two

French priests drew up plans for a submarine, though their ideas were entirely innocent of the practical problems of making a working vessel.

Garrett was born in Lambeth, London, a member of an evangelical Christian family. His father, a clergyman, moved the family to Moss Side in 1861, at about the time when the area was being transformed from a semi-rural township into a suburb of Manchester. The family constantly lived in poverty and debt, due not least to some unwise litigation entered into by his father and his father's considerable gift for making enemies. George himself was evidently a man of many talents, combining an interest in science (he carried out early experiments to develop a self-contained breathing apparatus) and great skill as a bare-knuckle boxer.

Despite winning a degree in science from Trinity College, Dublin, he was press-ganged by his father into becoming the curate in his church, mainly as a means of augmenting the family's disastrous finances. George combined his scientific interests with his curacy, and even took on a third job as a schoolmaster. On 8 May 1878 he took out a patent on a 'Submarine boat for placing torpedoes, etc.' (A torpedo in those days was any explosive device designed to be detonated under water, and so included things like mines). He set up a company, the Garrett Sub-Marine Navigation and Pneumataphore Company, based at 56 Deansgate, to promote the scheme. Eventually he raised enough money to build a 4½-ton prototype, which he named *Resurgam* (Latin for 'I shall rise again'). This was not practical as a warship, since the one-man crew had not only to operate the ballast tanks and hand-crank the propeller, but also to place or fire the torpedoes. However, the trials were sufficiently successful to encourage him to plan the full-sized (30-ton, 45ft long, steam-powered) *Resurgam II*. The press reported its trial as follows:

> A new submarine vessel, the invention of the Revd. George W Garrett of Manchester, was exhibited on Tuesday in the Wallesey Dock, before a large number of scientific and

other gentlemen. The object of the boat is to get near ships of war without being observed. The vessel is pointed at both ends. On the top there is a tower provided with windows, and there is a manhole by which the operator gets in or out of the vessel with ease.

Liverpool Weekly Mercury, 29 November 1879

Resurgam II was powered by a closed cycle steam engine, developed by American engineer Eugene Lamm. This superheated sufficient steam to power the craft for up to four hours, before the furnace was extinguished (so as not to consume the air supply) and it dived. However, the technology was not fully developed; the craft was stiflingly hot and the engine leaked fumes, leading to an illness christened 'steam submariner's lung'. Its other many design faults included difficulty in navigating, due to the lack of a periscope, and, most fatally, the fact that the hatch could not be properly sealed from the outside.

Nonetheless, Garrett decided to sail the craft from Merseyside to Portsmouth (since the Royal Navy refused to fund it without it undergoing trials there). They soon ran into trouble and put in at Rhyl for repairs. They left Rhyl in bad weather, with *Resurgam* now under tow by a steam yacht. This time, it was the steam yacht's turn to run into engine problems, and *Resurgam*'s crew left the submarine to help the yacht. Inevitably, the unsealed hatch on the submarine led to it taking on water and *Resurgam* sank to the bottom, never to 'resurg'. This led to Garrett's bankruptcy and the winding up of his company.

Garrett's perpetual absence from his clerical duties did not endear him to the parishioners of Moss Side, particularly when he got them to organise parish events that went to subsidise his submarine experiments. The rest of his life was no less colourful. He went on to design much larger submarines that saw service with the Greek, Swedish and Turkish navies (though these were called Nordenfeldt submarines, after their Swedish sponsor). He was also given a commission in the

Ottoman Navy and died penniless and starving in New York (none of which need trouble a book about Manchester). A replica of his craft can be seen near the Woodside terminal of the Mersey ferry in Birkenhead.

MANCHESTER MOTORS

Manchester has two early claims to fame in relation to the car industry. Before the First World War, the city became European home to the world's largest car maker and – all too briefly – the one that would become known as the world's finest motor manufacturer.

In 1884, a small firm of electrical and mechanical engineers was established in Cook Street, Hulme. Despite having only two years' formal education, the proprietor built up a business making dynamos, cranes, installing Liverpool's first electric street lighting, and much else (for example, he invented the bayonet light bulb fitting). In 1903, he bought himself his first car, a French Decauville, and he could not resist the temptation to tinker with it and improve it. By April 1904 he had progressed from tinkering to designing his own two-cylinder car. He then started to manufacture them in a small way and one of his models came to the attention of a car salesman, racing motorist and general adventurer. He was sufficiently impressed to arrange a meeting with the manufacturer and this historic occasion took place in the Midland Hotel in May, 1904. The manufacturer was Henry Royce and the car salesman was the Honourable Charles Rolls. The first Rolls-Royce car (as Rolls insisted they be called) was exhibited at the Paris salon in December of that year.

From the start, the company set itself a target of absolute excellence. What people might today call their mission statement was 'to turn out the best car in the world regardless of cost, and sell it to those people who could appreciate a good article and were willing and able to pay for it'. Their association with Manchester was brief – their Cook Street site did not have potential to expand and they started looking for another site in the Manchester area. Somewhere along the Stretford Road was being considered, but Derby Council lobbied them to relocate there and offered very favourable terms, and the company left Manchester in 1908. By that time they had developed from the two-cylinder prototype to the Silver Ghost, the 7-litre six-cylinder model which set the standard for luxury motoring until it ceased production in 1925. It is strange to think of the early models of this most luxurious marque of cars first seeing the light of day on the impoverished streets of Hulme.

Before the First World War, Manchester (or, more precisely, Trafford Park) was also home to Britain's largest volume car manufacturer. Henry Ford launched what was to be his most famous car, the Model T, at the Olympia Motor Show in London in October 1908. Over its nineteen-year production run, more than 15 million of them would be sold worldwide. From 1911, English supplies of the car were assembled at Trafford Park from components imported from America, although the British arm of the company soon developed a sizeable local input to the product – in particular, the bodywork was sub-contracted to a local company, Scott Brothers. Ford put a Briton, Percival Perry, in charge of the operation and he rapidly built up a nationwide network of around 1,000 dealers. Within two years, Trafford Park was turning out 7,310 Model Ts a year, at a time when Britain's largest home-grown car manufacturer, Wolseley, could barely manage 3,000.

The newspaper *Ford Times* gave this rationale for the selection of Trafford Park:

> Manchester, England was chosen for the site of this assembling plant, as it was necessary to have the factory accessible to the coast to facilitate transportation. The locality selected for the plant is Trafford Park, the largest manufacturing centre in Manchester. This property is adjoining the Manchester Ship Canal, which will greatly aid in the handling of freight.

Ford set new standards for industrial wages. The English operation learnt from the company's American experience that the dehumanising and dictatorial conditions of the production line that Ford pioneered led to huge levels of turnover and absenteeism. The company addressed this by paying unprecedentedly high wage rates (in England's case, £3 a week). The Model T remained in production until 1927, by which time Trafford Park had turned out well over 250,000 of them. Ford's association with Manchester did not long survive the demise of the Model T; they moved their operation (including many of their Manchester staff) to new headquarters at Dagenham in 1931.

THE TEXTILE REVOLUTION

The wider area of which Manchester forms the heart was the focus of Britain's cotton industry. In the eighteenth and early nineteenth centuries, a series of technological breakthroughs transformed it from a home-based craft industry to a factory-based giant that, by the early nineteenth century, supported around one in ten of the nation's population. A number of these innovations originated from within the Manchester area and all of them were applied there.

The developments started in about 1733. Up until that time, the larger looms required two people to operate them, until James Kay from near Bury came up with the flying shuttle. This meant that a single weaver could now operate the loom and vastly increased the productivity of the weaving industry. Like many innovators after him, Kay's invention made him neither rich nor popular. Manufacturers found ways of evading the royalties he was due on his invention, and irate weavers, who saw it threatening their livelihoods, attacked his house and forced him to flee abroad, where he died in poverty.

The increased productivity of the weavers now meant that it could take as many as sixteen cotton spinners to keep one weaver supplied with raw materials. In 1770, James Hargreaves, originally from Blackburn, patented the spinning jenny. This enabled one spinner to produce several threads at once, and would eventually increase their productivity by a hundredfold. Unfortunately, his invention coincided with a deep recession in the industry and hostility towards him from displaced workers again forced him to leave the area.

Samuel Crompton, a mill worker from Bolton, came up with a further improvement on the spinning machine, which became known as the mule. However, he was unable to patent it, and instead he hit upon the idea of raising a subscription for his efforts from the textile manufacturers, in return for which he would make his invention freely available to all. True to form, the manufacturers proved extremely ungenerous; despite the fact that, in Crompton's lifetime, some 4.2 million of his inventions were in use in Britain's mills, his subscription raised just £60. True also to form, his invention prompted riots among spinners in Manchester in March 1792. Crompton himself died in poverty in 1827.

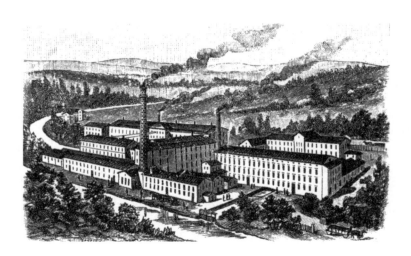

Last and quite possibly least, in a brief reference to Manchester's links with a specialist part of the textile industry, a third of the world's waterproof garments were once made at the Mackintosh plant in Chorlton-on-Medlock.

THE COMMUNIST REVOLUTION

Communism, the political creed that was arguably the most important in shaping the history of the twentieth century, can claim to have been conceived, if not born, in Manchester. Friedrich Engels was born into a wealthy German textile manufacturing family and was sent by his parents to work in Manchester, in the hope of curing him of his radical tendencies (which was rather like sending someone to the Sahara to cure them of sun-burn). On the way, he was introduced to Karl Marx and the pair of them used to meet in Manchester. Engels was writing his *Condition of the Working Class in England*, based on what he had seen in the poorer parts of Manchester, and Marx was shaping his ideas for the *Communist Manifesto* of 1848. They would sit and share their ideas in the reading room of Chetham's library (Engels lived at various addresses in Chorlton-on-Medlock and Marx took lodgings at Great Ducie Street, near the present-day site of Strangeways Prison). There can be little doubt that conditions in Manchester were influential in shaping the Manifesto; the historian Asa Briggs has suggested that, if Marx had focussed his attentions on Birmingham instead of Manchester, he would have been a currency reformer.

THE ATOMIC AGE

The atomic age can be said to have been born in Manchester. The Manchester scientist John Dalton (1766–1844) was the first to develop an atomic theory (that elements consisted of small indivisible particles of differing atomic weights) and was the first to devise a system for classifying them.

Ernest Rutherford was a New Zealand-born scientist who came to the University of Manchester from McGill University, Montreal, in 1907, to take up the Langworthy Chair of Physics. The following year he won a Nobel Prize, not for physics but for his work on the chemistry of radioactive substances. Radioactivity was at this time a very new area of science, one opened up by the work of Pierre and Marie Curie among others.

Rutherford assembled a talented team around him, including Hans Geiger (co-inventor of the Geiger counter, a device for detecting nuclear radiation) and Niels Bohr (himself a future

Nobel laureate and one of the team working on the wartime Manhattan project that would give the world the atomic bomb). In a laboratory in Bridgeford Street he detected the structure of an atom – a tiny nucleus at the centre of a group of orbiting electrons – and developed the concept of a half life for radioactive substances. Among other things, the latter gave science a basis for calculating the age of the earth, which turned out to be much greater than most scientists had thought. He first split the atom in 1917, in a nuclear reaction between nitrogen and Alpha particles, opening up all the far-reaching implications of the nuclear age. Rutherford remained with the university until 1919, before returning to the Cavendish Laboratory in Cambridge, where he had previously studied. No less than Albert Einstein described Rutherford as 'a second Newton' and, after his death in 1937, he was indeed buried close to Sir Isaac Newton in Westminster Abbey.

But to prove he did not get everything right, this is what he said about the potential for generating energy from atomic reactions:

> The energy produced by the breaking down of the atom is a very poor kind of thing. Anyone who expects a source of power from the transformation of these atoms is talking moonshine.

THE COMPUTER

Many people, and a number of Britons, from Charles Babbage and his nineteenth-century analytical engine to the wartime code-breakers at Bletchley Park, can claim to have contributed to the development of the modern computer. But it was work carried out at the University of Manchester in the 1940s that made the vital breakthrough that found its way into the first commercial computers. In December 1946, F.C. (Freddie) Williams was appointed as the university's Professor of Electro-Technics. He had previously worked at the Ministry of Supply's Telecommunications Research Establishment and he bought one of his former TRE colleagues, Tom Kilburn, in to work with him. Also present in the university's mathematics department was Max Newman, who had helped develop the code-breaking Colossus machine at wartime Bletchley Park.

Many people, particularly in America, had been working on computers – it was an idea whose time had come – but they were unable to get the storage mechanism to work. It was in this that the Manchester team made the big breakthrough. On 21 June 1948 their Small-Scale Experimental Machine (also known as 'Baby' – inappropriately, as it filled a large room) ran successfully for the first time. It was the world's first stored-program computer, and differed from others in that both the data and the program needed to analyse it were stored electronically. Previous models could only perform one function, or at best needed days of reconfiguring of the wiring to run a different program. Despite its very modest performance (the machine could initially handle just thirty-two words) this breakthrough was not lost on the scientific community or the media. The press called it (slightly prematurely) 'a marvel of our time; the "memory" machine that can solve the most complex mathematical problems'. Sir Henry Tizard, President of the British Association and scientific advisor to the government, also spoke highly of it. He said in July 1948 that it was:

... of national importance that the development should go on as speedily as possible, so as to maintain the lead that this country has thus acquired in the field of big computing machines, in spite of the large amount of effort and material that have been put into similar projects in America.

The government duly placed a £35,000 order with the Manchester firm Ferranti to develop the world's first commercially available computer, and in February 1951 the first production Ferranti Mark I was installed in Manchester University. IBM's first business computer did not appear until 1953, and it used the Manchester technology. Britain – and Manchester – remained at the forefront of computer technology for years to come. Ferranti also brought out the Atlas in 1962. Again designed by Manchester University, it was described as 'one of the fastest computers in the world at the time and also one of the most influential on successive generations.'

THE SATURDAY 'HALF-DAY HOLIDAY'

One of Manchester's odder claims to fame is that it is where the idea of working only a half day on Saturday originated. A survey in Manchester in the 1830s and '40s revealed that on Saturdays, as every other working day, it was 'quite common in the principal banks and warehouses to see every window illuminated up till nine, ten or eleven p.m., and the longest and sweetest of midsummer evenings often sank in the west before ever a door was locked and a lad set free.' Somebody called William Marsden launched a campaign in 1837 to secure half-day working hours on Saturdays as a universal right. By 1843 he got 441 Manchester businessmen to sign up to the proposal, despite fears on the part of some mill owners that workers would 'misapply the time they had in hand on the Saturday afternoon.' From these modest beginnings, the idea gradually won national acceptance. It has been suggested that Manchester's early espousal of the Saturday half-day helps to account for the city's strong sporting traditions, since it gave ordinary people the opportunity to play (or watch) sports, free from the inhibitions of either work or the Sabbath.

SOME MANCHESTER BRANDS

Boddingtons
The brewery at Strangeways was thought to have been founded in about 1778, though the first written reference to it dates from 1794. At that time it was run by Messrs Thomas Caistor and Thomas Fray, brewers and corn dealers. The brewery stood to the north of the River Irk, which then marked the outer limit of the town – being outside the

town had the tax advantage of avoiding paying Manchester Grammar School for the monopoly it had on the grinding of corn within the town. By 1828 it was trading as Hole, Potter & Harrison.

The Boddington family were long-established corn millers in Oxfordshire and, when business times grew hard in their area, John Boddington (born 1807) and his brother Henry (born 1813) decided to move north. They came to work for Hole, Potter & Harrison; John joining in 1831 in the accounts department and Henry the following year as a traveller. John soon left, setting up his own corn and provisions business in Ashton-under-Lyne in about 1835. Henry stayed on, advancing through the company to become a partner in 1848 at the age of thirty-four and its sole proprietor in 1853. The seventy-five-year-old company finally became known as Boddingtons and it first appears in a Manchester trade directory for 1854/5, offering 'pale ale, brewed especially for private families' and, by 1863 'light dinner beer 1s a gallon'.

They were producing 50,000 barrels a year by 1872, and 1877 saw the company move to new premises in Mary Street. By that time they were the largest brewer in Manchester, one of only thirty in the country to produce more than 100,000 barrels a year, which they sold through the seventy-one public houses they owned. Despite this growth, the Boddington family found time to be leaders of civic life in Manchester, being major promoters of the Manchester Ship Canal and trustees of many local charities.

The company has suffered reverses along the way. In 1891, two explosions of malt dust at the brewery led to the remodelling of part of the premises, and the brewery was badly damaged in the December 1940 air raids, putting it out of action for seven months. After the war, the company felt vulnerable to takeover and they established a trading agreement with Whitbread, under which they would sell each other's products. Over 130 years of Boddington control came to an end in 1989 when Ewart Boddington retired and, in October of that year, Whitbread took them over. They expanded the brewery's production from 200,000 barrels to 600,000 by 1994 and launched an advertising campaign that would turn the brand into a national one (albeit one leaning heavily on its Manchester roots).

Whitbread were, in their turn, taken over by Interbrew UK in 2000. Within two years they tried to close the Strangeways brewery but local opposition prevented them from doing so until 2005, when 227 years of brewing came to an end.

What was sold as Boddington's cask ale subsequently came from the Hyde's brewery in Moss Side.

Granada

Alexander Bernstein's first venture into show business, the Edmonton Empire Music Hall, was founded in 1908. By 1920, Bernstein had a growing chain of places of entertainment, including cinemas and theatres. In that year, his second son Sidney had gone walking in Spain and had arrived one snowy night at Granada. He explored the city and was captivated by it and its Alhambra Palace. The company was at that time searching for a suitably exotic name for its chain of venues and they settled upon Granada. The business later diversified into motorway services, bingo halls and – what it is best known for today – television. In the 1960s, television rental was big business and the company had a chain of some 200 television rental shops. These were given a big boost by the arrival of colour television. In 1970 there were only 100,000 colour television sets in use in the country but this number grew to 12 million by 1978. Many of these were rented and Granada was a market leader in renting them out.

Their first attempt to get into actual broadcasting dates back to 1948. Sidney and his brother Cecil applied for a licence to operate a closed-circuit television arrangement that would film West End shows on the last night of their run and show them for one night only on large screens in cinemas. The application was refused.

The Television Act of 1954 signalled the arrival of commercial television, and Granada decided to bid to become one of the programme contractors. They chose to bid for the northern region franchise, rather than any of the others, on the basis of two maps – showing population density and rainfall! They won the bid, but only secured broadcasting rights for five days a week. A derelict site in the centre of Manchester was chosen for the headquarters and Ralph Tubbs – one of the architects responsible for the Festival of Britain site – was chosen to build it. Large numbers of staff were needed to run the fledgling company and most of them needed to be trained from scratch. New transmitters had to be constructed at Winter Hill and Emley Moor and they began broadcasting in 1956.

At first the signs were not promising; viewing figures were not up to expectations, advertisers were pulling out and losses were being made at the rate of £20,000 per week. But Granada persevered and stuck to its policy of going for quality. They appointed Sir Thomas Beecham as their first musical consultant, and one of their first interviews was with the painter most associated with the north – L.S. Lowry. In 1960 they took another gamble in launching a soap opera set in a northern city back street. The other regions would not initially broadcast it, believing it to be too parochial, but I understand *Coronation Street* eventually attracted quite a number of viewers.

Sir Kenneth Clark, the former chairman of the Independent Television Authority, wrote in 1958:

> We did not quite see how much Granada would develop a character which distinguishes it most markedly from the other programme companies and from the BBC. This character may be described as immediacy – Granada believes in today.

Vimto
In 1908 John Noel Nichols set up business as a wholesale druggist and herb importer, with financial help from his family. In the days before a National Health Service, calling upon the services of a doctor was an expensive luxury for many people and they would turn instead to a herbalist or other alternative provider as a first source of help. Herbalists were also active in the temperance movement, offering herbal drinks as an alternative to the intoxicants found on licensed premises (and sometimes even as a replacement for altar wine in church services). Today, it is also used by film companies as a replacement for wine, in order to keep their actors sober

through repeated takes. It was in an attempt to produce such a drink that Nichols and his colleagues stumbled upon the recipe for Vimto.

Nichols' first premises were at 48 Granby Row, close to the University of Manchester's Institute of Science and Technology. He did not stay there long, moving in 1910 to larger premises in Salford. But the link with Manchester was restored in 1971 when they established premises in Wythenshawe.

The name Vimto was registered as a trademark in the medicines class on 14 December 1912, where it was described as 'a beverage for human use, not alcoholic, not aerated, and not medicated.' The formula has always been a closely guarded secret, known only to two people, and the company will only tell you that it contains 'about 29 ingredients'. They have assiduously protected their rights; as early as 1915 they prosecuted the Berni Brothers of Bargoed in Wales for selling imitation Vimto. It is perhaps best known today as a fizzy drink, but the company has only marketed it themselves as such since 1969 (prior to that, it was sold as a concentrate, to which fizzy water could be added).

During the war years, national branded soft drinks like Vimto disappeared entirely and manufacturers were restricted to catering for a local market. Vimto was sold under generic labelling as a 'Speciality Flavoured Cordial', though aficionados within the Manchester catchment area would have known they were getting the real thing.

Just as Campbell's soup has been immortalised by Andy Warhol, so Vimto is commemorated in a work of art. In 1992 a sculpture in stained oak was erected close to where the company's original premises stood. It showed a giant bottle of Vimto and a selection of fruits that might (or might not, it is a secret after all!) be in the drink. And the name? It seems to come from the idea that it gives you vim and vigour, as this 1950s advertising slogan suggests: Vitality! Vivacity! Vimto!

The Guardian

The *Manchester Guardian* has its origins in a court case held in Lancaster in March 1819, in which John Edward Taylor was acquitted of criminally libelling the leader of the Manchester Tories, John Greenwood. Taylor was the son of a Quaker Minister who was also the headmaster of a school in Manchester. After attending school, Taylor went into the cotton business, where he worked his way up to become a partner in a cotton manufacturer and then a merchant. But Taylor's real interest lay in public life – he was a reformer at a time when the repressive governments of the day made this a dangerous thing to be. He got into writing political articles for the *Manchester Gazette*, an outlet for radical middle-class opinion, but it was the Peterloo Massacre that triggered the events leading to the court case. Taylor became the *Times'* temporary correspondent covering the event after their regular correspondent, John Tyas, got arrested on the day. His carefully balanced account of these tragic events secured them a wider national audience than they might otherwise have attracted. This, and a series of pamphlets he subsequently produced on the massacre for the *Manchester Gazette*, led to the allegation of libel.

On the way back from Lancaster, it was put to Taylor that what was needed was a powerful newspaper to articulate these views. Eleven backers were found to put up a total of £1,050, premises were rented at 29 Market Street and, on 5 May 1821, the first edition of the *Manchester Guardian and British Volunteer* appeared, price 7*d* (most of which was government stamp duty, designed to discourage the circulation of radical views). The paper's prospectus was published in advance:

> The MANCHESTER GUARDIAN will commence its course with a very considerable circulation. It has secured an extensive and valuable patronage throughout the surrounding districts, among the classes to whom, more especially, advertisements are generally addressed; and whilst its Conductors respectfully solicit the support of advertisers both in this and the neighbouring towns, they confidently assure them, that it will offer a most eligible medium for giving extensive publicity to their notices.

But at the same time the paper would support a consistent character:

> ... for sincere and undeviating attachment to rational liberty ... It will zealously enforce the principles of civil and religious Liberty, the most comprehensive sense of those terms; it will warmly advocate the cause of reform; it will endeavour to assist in the diffusion of just principles of political economy; and to support without reference to the party from which they emanate, all serviceable measures ... We are the enemies of slander ... and we strongly believe that it will be by industry and careful attention, rather than on any other terms, that we will be able to support those who are aiming so hard at public improvement.

The initial print run was just 1,000 copies, rising to 3,000 by 1825. For the first fifteen years the *Manchester Guardian* was published weekly. It then became twice weekly and only became a daily paper in 1855, when the removal of the hated stamp duty enabled the price to be reduced to 1*d*.

Taylor married his cousin Sophia Russell Scott and in 1871 her nephew Charles, then a student at Oxford, joined the paper. Within a year he was made its editor at the age of twenty-six, a post that he would hold for the next sixty years. By 1907 he also became the paper's proprietor. The *Guardian* was, from its first edition, a campaigning newspaper and Scott continued this tradition throughout his editorship. Over the years the paper supported the Anti-Corn Law League, the 1857 Divorce Bill, equal rights for Catholics, women's suffrage, home rule for Ireland, the Secret Ballot Act of 1872 and the creation of a homeland for the Jews. At the same time, they were strongly opposed to: Abraham Lincoln and the Unionist cause in the American Civil War; the Boer War and the Suez campaign of 1956. Neither the paper nor its editors were afraid to make themselves unpopular in the causes they championed.

Scott died in 1932, and from 1936 the ownership of the paper was vested in the Scott Trust (a move originally to avoid possible crippling death duties, but one which also freed the paper from the undue influence of any future proprietor). Increasingly over the years the paper became a national, rather than a provincial, one. The name *Manchester* was dropped from its title in 1959; it began printing in London in 1961, and in 1964 the editorial headquarters were removed to London, though they still retained their Manchester premises, by now relocated to Deansgate.

2

FUN, FUN, FUN!

Morally offensive, socially subversive and a general impedi-
ment to progress.

One Victorian mill-owner's view of
working-class leisure activities.

How have Mancunians enjoyed themselves over the years?
Let's look at a few of the ways.

PLEASURE GARDENS

For almost 200 years, ornamental gardens open to the public
have entertained the people of Manchester.

Spring Gardens

There was once a Spring Gardens in Manchester at some time
before 1729. It was somewhere near what is known today as
Fountain Street and is remembered by a street name.

Vauxhall Gardens

Robert Tinker (1766–1836) was, by 1797, the proprietor of
the Grape & Compass Coffee House and Tea Gardens, in
what today seems an unlikely beauty spot – the banks of the
River Irk at Collyhurst. He changed its name to the Elysian
Gardens and dressed it with 3,000 coloured lights, promising
an evening 'at once intellectual, rural and delightful', complete

with singers and a band, and all for the admission price of 1s 6d. In 1814 he changed its name to the Vauxhall Gardens, after its more formal London counterpart, but locals by now knew it as Tinker's Gardens. It offered floral gardens, concerts and sporting events, a zoological gardens and horticultural wonders including, in 1814, a cucumber 7ft 8in long, not surprisingly promoted as 'the greatest curiosity of its kind nature ever produced in this kingdom'. Other regular attractions were the early balloon ascents. The promotional material for the August 1827 Royal Coronation balloon ascent says the gardens 'are so happily disposed by nature as to form a complete amphitheatre' to afford 'uninterrupted observance of every preliminary preparation.'

The year after Tinker's death, his gardens faced new competition in the form of those at Belle Vue, but they continued in business until 1852. As an aside, the name Vauxhall has medieval origins. The original gardens in London were built on land which once housed Fulk's Hall, the home of Falkes de Breauté, a medieval mercenary who was given the land for services to King John in the thirteenth century. Fulk's Hall changed over the years to 'Vauxhall', and an ironworks of that name later located there. It was there, too, that the first Vauxhall cars were made – the griffin emblem on the Vauxhall badge is part of Falkes' medieval coat of arms.

Pomona Gardens

The Pomona Gardens were another of Tinker's rivals, just across the boundary in Salford, near Ordsall Hall. They were named after the Roman goddess of fruit trees, gardens and orchards, but were originally called the Cornbrook Strawberry Gardens. The gardens (formerly to a private house) were opened to the public in the 1830s and other attractions, such as a zoological garden, were added later. At one time they had the largest ballroom in Britain and political rallies and leisure events could attract crowds of up to 100,000. Disraeli addressed an audience of 28,000 in one of the halls there.

The Pomona Gardens were a popular venue for Victorian Mancunians, many of them travelling there by boat. They would board it from the Cathedral Steps (as their name suggests, wooden steps leading down from Victoria Street near the cathedral). In the early days, the trip would have been something of a rural idyll, looking out over the Trafford Park woodlands, farms, orchards and a beauty spot called Throstlenest. But creeping industrialisation and the growing pollution of the river itself gradually made the journey less charming and more of an endurance test. The coming of the Manchester Ship Canal gave the public a new reason for taking the boat trip (giving views of the ocean-going ships in port) but also spelt the end for the Pomona Gardens. They were swallowed up in 1888 into what became the Pomona Docks, serving the Ship Canal. The loss of the gardens did not end the popularity of the river trips and, in the first half of 1897 alone, over 200,000 went to see the wonders of the Ship Canal. But the Cathedral Steps were closed in 1906. They stood just below where the rivers Irk and Irwell met, at one of the narrowest points in the River, and the introduction of a jetty at this point made the likelihood of flooding worse.

White City, Hulme

The Manchester Botanical and Horticultural Society was set up in 1827, one of its aims being to create a pleasure garden for the benefit of the general public. One of the purposes of this was to cool any revolutionary ardour among the working classes, just eight years after the Peterloo Massacre. As the society put it: 'What can be a more delightful relaxation to a Lancashire mechanic than an hour or two in a garden? What an escape from the pestiferous politics of the times.' The society was directed by the eminent scientist John Dalton to a site in Stretford, near modern day Old Trafford, where the prevailing wind would blow enough of the town's pollution away to give the plants a sporting chance. The gardens would be the site for the Art Treasures Exhibition of 1857 and an even more popular exhibition of Art, Science and Industry to mark Queen Victoria's Golden Jubilee in 1887.

By 1907 the popularity of the gardens was waning and part of the site was let to Messrs Heathcote and Brown, who undertook to provide 'a pleasure garden of the highest class'. They promised to scour the parks and fairgrounds of Europe and America to find the latest novelties (which they did in just ten weeks). A water chute and big dipper were among the attractions they brought back with them. The amusement park lasted until 1928, at which time it was decided to sell off the remainder of the site to enable the construction of a stadium and racing track. This played host to a variety of events, from athletics and greyhound racing to speedway and stock cars, until its closure and replacement by a retail park in 1982.

The only parts that survive to this day are the original entrance to the gardens and the name White City. This appears to have been quite a common name for pleasure gardens – others were to be found at Hull and Onchan on the Isle of Man, for example. Does the original come from the name given to the stadium built for the 1908 London Olympics (which opened at about the same time as Manchester's amusement park)? This was located in an area of Hammersmith that was open fields until just before then, but was used to house various trade exhibitions. The white stone-clad exhibition buildings were christened the White City by visitors, and the nickname transferred to the Olympic stadium and to the area as a whole.

Belle Vue

For many years Manchester's best-known leisure destination, Belle Vue was the brainchild of a Nottingham-born man, John Jennison. In 1826 he was working as a jobbing gardener when he decided to open the garden to his house as an attraction. They were known as Jennison's Gardens, or the Strawberry Gardens. This soon became a full-time activity for him, as he added a menagerie and a public house to the facilities. The business came to the attention of an entrepreneur named George Gill, who persuaded Jennison to expand by leasing a 35-acre site between Hyde Road and the Stockport Road. The site, previously used for occasional leisure events, was known as the Belle Vue Tea Gardens. The business flourished until new competition emerged from the Manchester Zoological Gardens at Higher Broughton in 1838. Then the Manchester to Birmingham Railway sliced through his site, cutting off access from the Stockport Road, after which recession drove Jennison into bankruptcy.

Unable to find another taker for the site, his creditors allowed Jennison to continue trading, at which point he had a dramatic reversal in fortunes. The recession also killed off some of his

competition and the railway company built Longsight station right next to Belle Vue. Far from cutting him off, the railway now allowed him to tap a huge hinterland of new customers. By 1843, Jennison was free of debt. From there, his zoological collection steadily grew and a range of new attractions was added, from a fireworks lake and island to a natural history museum. His family gradually took over the running of the business as Jennison's health failed (he died in 1869). By the turn of the twentieth century the gardens occupied 68 acres, with another 97 bought or leased next to the site, housing a circus ring, fairground, kinematograph and a roller-skating rink. One of their less conspicuous successes were their range of water ices, which were made from the polluted waters of their Great Lake (itself fed from the Stockport Canal) and which were the source of much food poisoning.

During the First World War, Belle Vue was turned over to military use. Soldiers drilled there and aircraft parts were assembled in the King's Hall and the roller skating rink. A munitions factory was built next to the athletics track. The fireworks displays continued, but now they depicted scenes from the western front. By the end of hostilities the place was in a run-down state and there was even talk of Manchester City FC acquiring it to build their new ground. But instead a promoter of fairgrounds and amusements, John Henry Iles, took it over in 1925. He built an entirely new amusement park and added additional attractions like wrestling, speedway and a Christmas circus. One of its star attractions was a roller coaster named The Bobs. Constructed by an American engineer, Harry Traver, and completed in 1929, The Bobs offered record-breaking velocity down its first incline (it ceased operating and was sold for scrap in 1970). In addition to these successful ventures, Iles also had his failures – chariot racing, baseball, midget car racing and rugby union were not popular, and Iles' ill-advised attempts to enter the film industry eventually bankrupted him.

Parts of Belle Vue were again commandeered for military use during the Second World War, though it continued to be important as a leisure centre as part of the government's policy of Holidays at Home. One new leisure activity was introduced; the Halle Orchestra, bombed out of the Free Trade Hall, found a temporary home at Belle Vue from 1941 to 1951. Post-war Britain was starved of leisure activities and the venue enjoyed another period of boom. More new facilities were added (including robots, waxworks and mock gunfights in 'Dodge City') and in 1956 it was bought by the Forte Group. But by now, television was starting to have a real impact on visitor numbers. In January 1958 the Great Ballroom was destroyed by fire and efforts to introduce new attractions could not stem the decline in visitor numbers. It finally closed, despite public protests and a 50,000-signature petition, in September 1977. The local press celebrated its passing as 'a place of entertainment and amusement … one of the most remarkable institutions of which Manchester or indeed any other city or town in the kingdom can boast'.

THE ART TREASURES EXHIBITION 1857

Two things provided the inspiration for Manchester's Art Treasures Exhibition. First, 1851 saw the landmark of the Great Exhibition at the Crystal Palace in London. It was the first international exhibition of the works of industry of all nations, and was visited by over 6 million people. A good many Mancunians made the journey and a number of them came back with the idea that Manchester should stage something similar – the town had been hosting exhibitions on a smaller scale since the 1830s. The second inspiration was the publication of a book by Dr Gustav Waagen, the Director of the Royal Gallery in Berlin, in 1854. This made the point that much of the best art in Britain lay unseen, in private collections. These two items came together in the mind of a Manchester cotton manufacturer, J.C. Deane, who persuaded the mayor and others to back an important cultural event in Manchester (the mayor agreed on the basis that no public funding would be forthcoming for it). Over 100 private subscribers were found to underwrite the cost of a suitable building. The idea was that the great and the good would be asked to lend items from their private art collections to be exhibited.

The project got a valuable boost in May 1856 when Prince Albert granted it royal patronage, on condition that any profits should be used for the welfare of local citizens. The Queen also volunteered to visit it. A site for the event was found, in the White City pleasure gardens near Old Trafford cricket ground.

Requests to art collectors for the loan of exhibits (led by George Scharf, later the first Director of the National Portrait Gallery) met with a mixed response. Some questioned what Manchester (an industrial powerhouse, but regarded as something of a cultural backwater) was doing, taking an interest in the arts. They suggested that the town should concentrate on its spinning and weaving. Others, like the Earl of Ellesmere, wrote the organisers a list (from memory) of the items he would let them have. Eventually some 16,000 art objects and 1,812 paintings were assembled. On 5 May 1857 Albert led a grand procession through the town to the exhibition site, and the Queen visited it the following month. They were followed by many members of the artistic establishment and suddenly Manchester was being taken seriously by them. The *Illustrated London News* said that Manchester 'hurls back upon her detractors the charge that she is too deeply absorbed in the pursuit of material wealth to devote her energies to the finer arts', and the *Times* called it 'the scene of an event almost unique in the history of art in England or perhaps in the world'. In addition to the exhibition, there were lectures on the arts by John Ruskin and other luminaries, and music provided by what would eventually become the Halle Orchestra.

There were a few critics – one Manchester clergyman labelled some of the exhibits indecent and feared the influence that the pictures from 'Romish countries' would exert. Others criticised the presentation of the exhibits, but most regarded it as a huge success. When it closed in October, it had been seen by 1,336,715 paying customers; nothing had been stolen or damaged and it even made a profit. In addition to all the culture, Manchester also widened its appeal by offering entertainment of a less-demanding nature, including an exhibition of Madame Tussaud's new waxworks and Professor Anderson, the Great Wizard of the North, who offered 'embellishments of the costliest character, apparatus perfectly novel, miracles of mechanism and mystic means of mirth.'

THE HALLE ORCHESTRA

Manchester is home to Britain's oldest orchestra and probably the fourth oldest in the world. Its founder, Charles Halle, was born in Westphalia in 1819, studied piano in Paris from 1836, and began to make a name for himself on the concert platform until the revolutions in mainland Europe in 1848 drove him to England. He in turn encouraged his friend Chopin to come over and perform in Manchester. Chopin hated performing in public at the best of times, and was at this time dying of consumption. His distaste for the reception he got in Manchester nearly led to Halle quitting the town for a position in Bath, but Herman Leo, a calico printer and part-time musical impresario, persuaded him that Manchester was ripe for a transformation in its musical tastes.

Since the 1770s Mancunians had subscribed to seasons of Gentlemen's Concerts. Mendelssohn had conducted them in a performance of his *Elijah* in 1847, and was apparently less than impressed with the orchestra. Halle took them over in 1850, introducing new musicians and cheaper tickets than the standard five guineas for the season.

The organisers of the Art Treasures Exhibition in 1857 paid Halle £4,515 to create an entirely new orchestra to perform daily to its visitors, and this led to Halle organising a series of weekly concerts at the Free Trade Hall from 1858 onwards. By the latter part of the nineteenth century, the orchestra had a reputation for excellence throughout Europe that enabled them to attract some of the top artistes of the day. Grieg himself played his piano concerto with them, they gave the first British performance of Berlioz's *Symphony Fantastique*, the world premiere of Elgar's first symphony and some of the first British performances of symphonies by Brahms and Dvorak.

Halle died in 1895 and such was the reputation of his orchestra that they were able to appoint Hans Richter, principal conductor of the Vienna Opera and the Vienna Philharmonic Orchestra, in his stead. He was the first in a long line of distinguished holders of the post, which included Sir Thomas Beecham (1914–17), Sir Hamilton Harty (1920–33) and Sir John Barbirolli (1943–70). Many of the orchestra were called up for military service during the First World War and their places taken by women. In the inter-war years, Sir Hamilton Harty outraged sections of public opinion by his efforts to get rid of them all.

For many years, the orchestra made its home at the Free Trade Hall, until this was largely destroyed in the 1940 bombing raid. It was rebuilt by 1951, but the Halle finally moved to their new purpose-built home, the Bridgewater Hall, in 1996.

FOOTBALL

Manchester can at present truly claim to be Britain's premier football city. But the origins of the two main Manchester clubs were far more humble.

The Heathens – Newton Heath FC

In 1878 a group of workers on the Lancashire & Yorkshire Railway decided to form a football team. They called it Newton Heath after their place of work and their matches were played on a ground at North Road (later the site of Moston Brook School). By 1892 the side had advanced to the point where they were invited to join the First Division of the Football League. At the end of their first season their landlords, the Dean and Canons of Manchester, insisted that they should stop charging for admission to their matches and they were forced to move to Bank Street in Clayton (near to what is today the site of the velodrome), where the surrounding chemical works and railways created a poisonous atmosphere for any kind of athletic activity.

The club did not flourish; they were relegated in 1894 and by 1902 were so in debt that the bailiffs used to gather around the turnstiles and seize the gate money, leaving the club with nothing to pay the players' wages. But they were rescued by a wealthy brewer, John Henry Davies, who first learned about the club when a dog, being used to advertise a fund-raising event, strayed into his house. He transformed the club, changing their colours from green and yellow to red and white and their name from Newton Heath to Manchester United (the name was almost Manchester Celtic or Manchester Central). By 1906 they had been promoted back into the First Division and their Bank Street ground had a capacity of 50,000.

In 1909 they won the FA Cup and Davies decided to move them to a new ground, five miles away. He did so just in time; they played their last game at Bank Street in January 1910 and, a few days later, the stand blew down in a storm. Their new home was a £60,000 stadium with an 80,000 capacity at Old Trafford. It was one of the wonders of the footballing world and was home to the 1915 FA Cup final, among other events.

United again fell on hard times between the wars. In 1931 gates fell to an average of 12,000 and the club was once again relegated. A new benefactor was needed, and one appeared in the shape of James Gibson, a local manufacturer of army uniforms, who paid off their £30,000 debt. The ground was bombed and seriously damaged in March 1941, and United had to share Maine Road with Manchester City, in an arrangement that lasted until well after the war. In fact, it was at City's ground that United secured the record for the Football League's largest crowd – 83,260 for their match against Arsenal in 1948.

A decade later and the club captured the imaginations of the nation for all the wrong reasons – in February 1958 they played a European fixture in Belgrade. On the way back, their aeroplane stopped to refuel at Munich, but it crashed when it tried to take off again. Twenty-one people were killed, including seven of the players (an eighth, Duncan Edwards, died in hospital fifteen days later) and their manager Matt Busby was seriously injured. But within two weeks the side were back in business, fielding two of the survivors from the crash and several who were more accustomed to playing for the third or youth teams. This scratch eleven managed to beat Sheffield Wednesday 3–0 in their first cup tie, and went on to reach that year's FA Cup final.

Since then, the side has enjoyed a string of Cup and League successes, including two European club championships.

West Gorton FC

In 1880 a church sporting club in east Manchester changed its allegiance from cricket to soccer. For its first few years, the club had something of a nomadic and confused existence, playing at a variety of grounds and under several different names (West Gorton, Gorton and Ardwick). By 1887 their home ground was a piece of industrial wasteland at Hyde Road, again surrounded by railways and industrial premises. Despite their location, they were invited in 1892 to become one of the founder members of Division Two of the Football League. Within two years, Ardwick FC had gone bankrupt, only to be reborn as Manchester City. They were more successful in their new guise, winning the Second Division championship in 1899 and the FA Cup in 1904. Shortly after this success (and hopefully unrelated to it), no less than seventeen of their players, along with their manager and chairman, were suspended for match-fixing offences.

In 1920 the stand at their insalubrious ground burned down and, with the lease on the ground itself about to expire, they decided to relocate. They got a cheap deal on 16 acres of former clay-pit in Moss Side and set out to build the largest ground anywhere in Britain (other than Wembley, itself then under construction). Soon they were regularly playing in front of crowds of more than 70,000, and a cup tie against Stoke in 1934 drew the largest crowd ever seen at any domestic game, other than FA Cup finals – 84,569.

But City's next golden age wasn't until the 1960s and early '70s, when they won the First Division championship for the second time in 1968 (the first was in 1937), the FA Cup in 1969 and the European Cup Winners' Cup in 1970. Their association with Maine Road ended in 2003, when they moved to a new 48,000 seat stadium in east Manchester, not far from where both they and Manchester United started out. They were bought by extremely wealthy interests from Abu Dhabi in 2008, making them one of the world's richest football clubs, and a new period of success beckoned, lifting the FA Cup in 2011 and winning the Premier League in 2012.

MANCHESTER RACES

These were held on Kersal Moor (about 2½ miles from Manchester) during Whitsun Week, the first meeting taking place in June 1729. From 1733, subscriptions were invited to help promote the event, and crowds of up to 100,000 reportedly attended. The promoters of the event were the Byrom family but one of their number, Edward Byrom, was one of its leading opponents. He was a staunch Methodist and associate of John Wesley, and he published a pamphlet calling for the event to be discontinued. Other members of the church thought Byrom's position unduly po-faced and a representative of the Collegiate Church suggested that he:

> ... might have found a subject more obnoxious than horse racing ... when our cities swarm with intemperance, lewdness and debauchery and our presses groan with atheistical and immoral authors. When fraud, violence and corruption are countenanced by such powerful numbers, and authorised by such high examples, as to give a kind of sanction to vice and injustice.

The authorities were certainly uneasy about horse racing generally, regarding the meetings as the cover for all sorts of crime and drunken excess. The notorious highwayman Dick Turpin was said to have been an enthusiastic follower of the racing at Kersal Moor in the 1730s; he and his girlfriend (the latter disguised as a boy) were said to have been regular visitors. In 1740 parliament introduced an Act 'to restrain and prevent the excessive increase in horse racing' (it was largely ignored). But one thing horse racing did do was to distract the masses from any more serious political protest and, with this in mind, Manchester races were allowed to go ahead within days of the Peterloo Massacre. They served their purpose, giving the authorities effectively a three-day armistice at a time of great tension. From 1830, race meetings quickly became some of the favourite leisure destinations for the new army of rail travellers. Mancunians would travel in large numbers to the racecourses at Liverpool and Newton-le Willows, with

Newton even getting its own dedicated branch line within two years of the Manchester to Liverpool railway opening.

One aspect of horse racing that the authorities were not prepared to tolerate was the growth in off-course betting, often in luxurious betting shops. Fears that gambling would lead large numbers of working men into poverty or crime led to them being banned in 1853.

Racing continued at Kersal Moor until 1847, when the course was moved across the River Irwell to a site known as Castle Irwell. It moved again in 1867, this time to Weaste. This site was in turn redeveloped in 1901 and racing returned to Castle Irwell. This course finally closed in November 1963 and the Manchester area has since been without its own racecourse, though there was talk in 2004 of developing a new £100 million facility in Greater Manchester.

MANCHESTER AND THEATRE

Manchester's first permanent theatre opened in 1753 in Marsden Street. Its first performance was a charitable one, to raise funds for the recently-opened infirmary. One gets the impression that its finances were initially a little uncertain – they advertised that a concert in April 1760 would begin 'at six o'clock in the evening to whatever company there may happen to be in the house'. They also seemed to glory in the amateurish nature of some of the attractions:

> … between the parts of the concert, for the further amusement of the Ladies and Gentlemen, will be presented, gratis, a Tragedy called *Theodosius*, or the *Force of Love*; all the characters exhibited by persons without hire, gain or reward.

Despite this, the enterprise took off. Boxes were added, and by 1775 the theatre had outgrown its premises and a new building, the Theatre Royal, was erected by public subscription.

Not all Mancunians appreciated the theatre. The Palace theatre at the corner of Oxford Street and Whitworth Street began life in 1891 as the Palace of Varieties Music Hall. It did so in the teeth of fierce opposition from local Methodists, who feared it might corrupt public morals. The Gaiety Theatre on Peter Street was actually closed down by the council's Watch Committee, on grounds of obscenity.

Another venue that started life as a music hall was the Ardwick Green Empire, 'a handsome and well-appointed building' at the junction of Hyde Road and Stockport Road. It was one of the products of the great theatrical entrepreneur Oswald Stoll. Charlie Chaplin and Marie Lloyd both appeared there, and one 1947 variety show has (at the very bottom of the bill) two young acts by the names of Max Bygraves and Frankie Howerd. From 1935 the venue was renamed the New Manchester Hippodrome, after the original Hippodrome closed. In November 1958 the venue hosted the area final of Carroll Levis' *Star Search* programme, in which unknowns got to pitch for stardom. One of the acts was what they might have called at the time 'a popular beat combo' called Johnny and the Moondogs. They failed to win the final, and so missed appearing on the televised show. But they went down rather better on their return to the city a few years later, by which time they had changed their name to the Beatles. The Empire/Hippodrome closed in 1961 and was finally demolished (after a fire) in 1964.

3

GHOSTS AND GHOULS

It will come as no surprise that a city as ancient and diverse as Manchester has its share of ghost stories and legends. Some of these are recounted below, although the author accepts no responsibility for their accuracy!

STRANGEWAYS PRISON

A hundred people were executed at Strangeways prison before hanging was abolished (the last of these, on 13 August 1964, was Gwynne Evans, who was one of the last two men in Britain to be executed). Staff working the night shift at the prison have reported seeing a mysterious figure in a dark suit, carrying a small briefcase. He is first seen just outside the condemned cell, then walks along B wing towards the central control area. When they have tried to follow him, the figure disappears, just before the steps leading up to the main office. Staff believe it to be the ghost of John Ellis, a Rochdale barber who doubled as the prison's hangman between 1901 and 1924, and who committed suicide in 1932. It was said that he never recovered from the distress he experienced at the hanging of Mrs Edith Thompson in 1923.

Another part of the prison, I2 landing, was used in the 1950s to house female prisoners awaiting the death sentence. One of these was the so-called Blackpool Poisoner, Mrs Louisa Merrifield. She had been hired as the carer to a seventy-nine-year-old widow, Sarah Ricketts, and, having got her to change her will in Merrifield's favour, fed her rat poison. She was executed on 18 September 1953. Both staff and inmates have subsequently reported seeing an apparition answering her description, walking along I2 landing then vanishing through the locked door of the condemned cell. They report experiencing a marked drop in temperature as she passes.

TOPLEY STREET, COLLYHURST

A building there was used by spiritualists until the caretakers mysteriously disappeared. Shortly afterwards, in about 1962, a local family with small children moved in. One of the children complained of being woken by 'an old man in black, swinging a watch-chain'. He was later joined by an old woman with 'a malicious look on her face'. Manchester Psychical Society were brought in to investigate. They recorded noises of glass breaking and furniture being moved, but could find no physical evidence to account for the noise. Animals refused to stay in the house; the family budgie died and an attempt to exorcise whatever was occupying the building failed. The building was later demolished.

MRS POTTER

Mrs Potter was murdered at 35 Northern Drive, Collyhurst. Two years later, she is said to have appeared to two children in the house, telling them to 'wait for me in this room' and touching one of them on the mouth. The children had to be treated for shock in hospital.

THE SWIVEL HOUSE

There was a property in Didsbury called the Swivel House, at one time occupied by an elderly bachelor, Sam Dean. He had made a fortune out of a kind of hand loom he had invented. When he died, no trace of his fortune was to be found, but what the new occupant of the house did find was that it was haunted by a beautiful female ghost. She wore old-fashioned clothes, red shoes, had powdered hair and a handkerchief tucked in her bosom. It is thought that she was the one-time lady friend of Sam, who had either robbed him of his fortune or knew too much about its whereabouts. It was claimed that a secret chamber had been found in one of the house's chimneys.

BOGGART HOLE CLOUGH

According to one nineteenth-century writer: 'Tread softly ... for this boggart clough, and see in yonder dark corners, and beneath projecting mossy stones, where the dusky sullen cave yawns before you ... there lurks a strange elf, the sly and mischievous boggart.' Boggarts are mischievous spirits that live in holes in damp places (to complete the explanation of the place-name, a clough is a northern term meaning a steep wooded ravine). They are said to be most common in

Yorkshire and Lancashire, in particular the swampy, mossy areas to the north of the Mersey. However, many of these areas have been drained, either for agriculture or development, depriving boggarts of their habitats and their food supply, which consisted of creatures trapped on the moss. Boggart Hole Clough is one area of their habitat that remains relatively untouched. Their mischief can take many forms – making things disappear, causing milk to go sour, dogs to go lame. They throw things about and shrink themselves, so as to enter the ears of horses and panic them into bolting. At night, they would enter one's bed and touch the sleeper with clammy hands or pull the bedclothes off them. In the past, they are said to have become such a nuisance that they have driven farmers from their land. The farmer George Cheetham was subject to these attacks in 1827, and he got to the point of packing up his worldly goods and leaving, until he discovered that the boggart had secreted himself among them and planned to accompany them to their new home. At this point, Cheetham decided he might as well stay where he was and be tormented there. There is some suggestion that this is all a Yorkshire tale that has been exported to Lancashire.

MANCHESTER CATHEDRAL

In the 1840s, a man saw his sister, Fanny, standing nearby. This surprised him, since he understood her to be many miles away. He called to her but she disappeared. Next day he learned that she had been killed in an accident, just at the time he had seen her.

PHANTOM HOUNDS

In 1825, a headless black hound was seen in the cathedral precincts. It leapt up and put its paws on the shoulders of a man named Drabble. Terrified, Drabble fled from the cathedral and down Deansgate, rushing into his house and diving (fully dressed, including boots) under his bedclothes.

On a clear moonlit night in 1957, a policeman patrolling near the junction of Spath Road and Holme Road, Didsbury, saw a mysterious dog crossing the lawn of an old house. It suddenly vanished, in a manner strange enough to cause the officer to return there in daylight to investigate. He found nothing except the moss-covered tombstone of a pet grave, inscribed 'Paddy. Died 2 September 1913'.

MANCHESTER TRANSPORT MUSEUM

A bus from Stockport is said to be haunted by the ghost of a young boy dressed in 1950s clothing. After his appearances were reported, the history of the bus was investigated, and it was indeed involved in an accident in Reddish, in which a young boy was killed.

DIDSBURY PARSONAGE

This had such a reputation for being haunted that servants refused to sleep in it and it was abandoned in 1850. Even the wrought iron gates to the parsonage gardens were referred to as 'the gates to hell'. But Alderman Fletcher Moss was not deterred by this reputation; he bought the parsonage in 1865 and lived in it for over forty years, apparently without any evil effect.

MANCHESTER AIRPORT

There have been a series of reported sightings of ghostly figures in the airport's Terminal 3 (opened 1989). The most common of these involves a male dressed as flight crew. The terminal is on the site of the building that was home to RAF 613 Squadron during the Second World War. Other ghostly happenings in the airport area include sightings of an old man, screams and other noises and equipment being mysteriously moved.

BLACKLEY HALL

The hall was built in the reign of Henry VIII, not far from the junction of Manchester and Rochdale Roads. It was said to have been haunted by the ghost of Old Shay, an eighteenth-century tenant and murder victim. He wandered through the house with a black dog 'making unearthly noises at the dead of night and taking liberties with the crockery ware and doors of the room'. The house was demolished in 1815.

SHAKESPEARE HOTEL, FOUNTAIN STREET

There has been a public house on this site since 1771, though the present building is understood to have been taken down from its original site in Chester and re-erected in Manchester in 1928. A young girl was murdered in a building that previously occupied the site. It is said that her ghostly figure can sometimes be seen at the top of the stairs. On one occasion, it appeared to be on fire.

RYLANDS LIBRARY

The silent figure of a lady is sometimes said to be seen in the upper gallery and the basement of the library. Inexplicable footsteps and the slamming of doors are heard, and ghostly hands have touched staff on the shoulder or tugged at their clothes.

HOUGH HALL, MOSTON

The January 1888 edition of *Cheshire Notes and Queries* carried a report dating back to around 1800, when the area around Moston was still open countryside. One Roderick Glossip was in the grounds of the hall early one morning when he encountered the ghost of a previous occupant of the hall, Captain Hough, mounted on his horse and surrounded by his equally ghostly pack of hounds.

SOME OTHER MANCHESTER GHOSTS

Not so much a ghostly visitation as a supernatural event was reported in **Blackley** in 1650. As the corn was being reaped, it appeared to bleed. Crowds gathered to witness the strange event.

A figure dressed in grey, thought to be a former cellar man, is said to be seen in the basement of the **Great Western Hotel, Moss Side**. His visits are said to be accompanied by a sudden drop in temperature.

A phantom monk is said to inhabit the cellar of the **Church Inn, Prestwich**, occasionally crying out 'Hello!' to anyone who would listen.

One resident of **Elsham Gardens, Gorton**, had a female 'friend' called Molly, who would wait in his room for him when they went out. Previous residents apparently moved out after seeing the ghost of a young boy there.

The **Palace Theatre** is said to be occupied by the ghost of a cleaner who died in the building.

Worsley Old Hall is said to be inhabited by the lime green ghost of a woman called Dorothy who re-enacts her death, falling down the stairs and breaking her neck.

The **Royal Exchange** theatre is said to have various ghosts, including a Victorian lady with 'a passion for drink' and the theatre's founding director, James Maxwell.

Hulme Hall was bought and demolished in 1845, to allow the construction of a railway. The hall was said to contain buried treasure, guarded by unearthly demons.

A former resident of **Heaton Hall** named Alice is said to frequent the building.

4

LAWLESS AND
DISORDERLY

The streets of Manchester have seen their fair share of conflict and violence over the years, as the following examples show.

CIVIL WAR COMES TO MANCHESTER

Manchester had the grim distinction of being the place where the first death of the Civil War occurred. The town had a strong puritan element in its population, and when leading Royalist Lord Strange arrived there a week before war was formally declared in August 1642, intent on acquiring the town's supplies of gunpowder, it provoked a gunfight in the streets. In the course of this, one Richard Percival, a linen weaver from Kirkmanshulme, was fatally wounded.

Within weeks of the outbreak of war Strange was back, at the head of 2,000 infantry, 300 cavalry and artillery. But the citizens had enough notice of his approach to fortify the outer limits of the town; they were assisted in this by a German professional soldier and military engineer, Johann Rosworm, who had taken up residence in the town. Strange's call for immediate surrender and free access to the town met with a predictably dusty response, and fighting broke out. The Royalists had by far the worst of the first engagement, losing (by one estimate) 120 men to the Mancunians' three.

After several days' fighting, in which the Royalists made little or no progress, Manchester's weather started to play a part. Unlike the townspeople, the Royalist forces had little or no shelter from the unrelenting rain, and their troops naturally began to get demoralised. Strange offered increasingly generous terms for surrender, all of which were rebuffed – the Mancunians said they would not hand over so much as a rusty dagger. Eventually, an exchange of prisoners was agreed, though the Royalists did not have enough to match those held by the Mancunians and were reduced to kidnapping non-combatants from the surrounding area to make up the numbers. The exchange completed, the Royalists retreated in confusion. The Mancunians strengthened their defences as a precaution against further attacks, but they were not needed.

Though they were militarily successful, the town was very hard hit by the disruption to trade caused by the war, not to mention the cost of maintaining a garrison in the town (until the latter was finally funded by the sequestration of Royalist estates). Collections were held in churches up and down the land for the relief of Manchester.

MANCHESTER AND THE PRETENDERS

Manchester was once again involved in attempts to overthrow the crown in 1715 and 1745, though it has to be said that the town's involvement was, on these occasions, much briefer and less whole-hearted than that of the Civil War. As we will see elsewhere in the book, there was a strong Jacobite element among the town's population, who supported the reinstatement of the deposed Stuart dynasty. Some of them would pay with their lives for their allegiance. One of its leading lights was a blacksmith, Tom Syddall, who was among those who destroyed the Cross Street Chapel in 1715 (on 10 June, the birthday of the former King James II). He was arrested for this and only liberated as the advancing Jacobite forces (supporting the son of the exiled former king, also called James) overran Lancaster. Spurred on by news that their leader had been proclaimed King James III in Manchester, and that support for the cause was mobilising throughout Lancashire, the Jacobites headed southwards, but only reached Wigan before they were routed by government forces. (Additional government forces were also sent to Manchester, to keep its troublesome population under control.) Syddall was among those captured and he was executed, his head being displayed on the Market Cross in Manchester.

Come 1745 and a new Stuart – Bonnie Prince Charlie – was the Young Pretender to the throne. He landed in Scotland with just a handful of men but began accumulating support as they moved south. The first Manchester saw of the advancing army was on 28 November, when one Sergeant Dickson, a drummer and a girl arrived in town and started recruiting Jacobite sympathisers. They had signed up 180 of them by the time the Young Pretender arrived, despite unsuccessful attempts by the anti-Jacobites among the population to have them arrested. The prince held court at the

house of local linen draper John Dickenson (thereafter known as the Palace). Charles had hoped to recruit a force of some 1,500 men from Manchester but, by the time he moved on, his Manchester Regiment numbered just 200–300.

None of the leading families of Lancashire openly sided with him. Some (including, it is thought, Manchester's Lords of the Manor, the Mosleys) were sympathetic but kept their involvement discreet. Some carefully arranged it so that, if needed, it would appear that their support had been extracted under duress and, according to the diary of Beppy Byrom, 'The Presbyterians are sending everything that's valuable away, wives, children and all, for fear of the rebels.' Some who signed up did so only because they had been unemployed and would equally happily have signed up for the other side had they offered employment first. The ambiguity of Manchester's attitude towards the Young Pretender is reflected in this epigram by John Byrom:

God bless the King! I mean our faith's defender
God bless – no harm in blessing – the Pretender
But who Pretender is, and who is King
God bless us all, that's quite another thing

Among those who did sign up for Prince Charlie for ideological reasons was another Tom Syddall, son of the Jacobite blacksmith. He had been just seven years old when his father had been executed in 1715. He marched away with the Jacobites as they headed south. This time they got as far south as Derby, before widespread desertions and advancing opposition forces made Charles turn around and head back to his Scottish stronghold. By the time he got back to Manchester, the anti-Jacobite elements were thoroughly in control and the town gave him a much more hostile reception. The Jacobite forces responded by looting and Charles tried to impose a £5,000 fine on the town (only half of which was paid). The Manchester contingent of the Jacobite forces were allocated the hopeless task of defending Carlisle as the rest of them continued their flight northwards, to the eventual massacre at Culloden. The Manchester contingent eventually surrendered and many paid with their lives. Among them was Thomas Syddall, whose head, like his father's, was displayed on a spike, this time at the Manchester Exchange.

FOOD RIOTS AND THE SHUDEHILL FIGHT

The rapid growth of Manchester brought with it some serious problems; recession and food shortages made it difficult to feed the new industrial settlements and, more particularly, the needs of the population far outstripped the ability of existing transport systems to supply them, at least at an affordable price. This last problem would only really be addressed by the coming of the railways. The result, from about 1750 onwards, was a series of food riots, for which the army often had to be called out to restore order. In June 1757, two women's protests against the price of potatoes escalated into sacks of them being overturned and looted in the market, and attacks on other food retailers. The arrest and imprisonment of the two women only resulted in a mob breaking them out of jail and going on a further rampage, and peace was only restored when some thirty special constables were appointed and a force of dragoons brought into the town.

That same November, more serious disorder broke out when rioters from Ashton-under-Lyne came into Manchester in search of food. They were initially driven off by a group of retired soldiers called the Invalids, who were based in the town, but returned two days later, still demanding cheap food. After they took a scythe to the High Sheriff, the Invalids intervened again and the warfare escalated to the use of firearms. Three of the rioters were killed and many more injured in the following two days' disturbances, before the dragoons (supported by two companies of infantry) arrived to restore order. These were the events that came to be known as the Shudehill Fight.

THE PETERLOO MASSACRE

In the years following the end of the Napoleonic wars, conditions for many of Manchester's citizens were desperate. The end of hostilities had released large numbers of people onto the labour market at a time when the city's staple textile industry was undergoing rapid technological change. Things were made worse by a government that was deeply repressive, reactionary and suspicious of the newly-urbanised working classes in the northern industrial towns and cities. The home secretary of the day, Henry Addington, Viscount Sidmouth, had a network of spies in these areas, who justified their existence by feeding him alarmist stories of imminent revolution. Sidmouth's fears were further justified (at least in his mind) when, in 1812, rioting between conservative and liberal elements broke out in Manchester, and was only put down by the use of military force. That same year also saw the last of the town's food riots.

In 1817, plans were made for a protest march to London, calling for (some fairly moderate) reforms. They were called the Blanketeers, from the makeshift bedding they carried strapped across their backs. The government had taken swingeing powers to prevent public protest meetings, but the Blanketeers sought to exploit a loophole in legislation passed during the reign of Charles I, under which groups of ten or less petitioners did not constitute 'a tumultuous assembly'. However, a crowd estimated at between 40,000 and 60,000 assembled in St Peter's Fields (the area around modern Peter Street) to see them off. The authorities read the Riot Act, tried to arrest the ringleaders and sent in the cavalry to attack both marchers and their unarmed supporters, one of whom was killed. Only one of the Blanketeers ever reached London, where he presented his petition to Lord Sidmouth, whose reaction to it was predictably dismissive.

Conditions were even worse by 1819, when a new and unlikely leader came to Manchester. Henry 'Orator' Hunt was from gentleman farming stock in Wiltshire, and came to

Manchester with a reputation (in the government's eyes) as a troublemaker. Plans were made for a political meeting in St Peter's Fields on 16 August. For their part, the government prepared for it by bringing in over 1,000 troops (cavalry and infantry), 400 or 500 constables and cannon.

On the day, the crowd was estimated at anything between 30,000 and 150,000. They were peaceful in their demeanour, which is more than can be said for the Manchester and Salford Yeomanry, an ill-trained and inexperienced militia drawn from elements in the civilian population who were as opposed to reform as the government. They led the way on horseback into the crowds to try and arrest the ringleaders. Their horses panicked, the crowd panicked, and the militiamen panicked and started laying into crowd with their swords. A conservative estimate put the casualty figures at eleven dead and about 420 wounded. It is thought many of the wounded either did not present themselves to the medical services for fear of further reprisals, or were refused treatment. We know, for example, that a weaver named James Lees went to a Dr Ransome for treatment of a sabre cut to his head after the event. Ransome asked him whether he had now had enough of meetings. When Lees said 'no', Ramsome immediately threw him out of the surgery, untreated.

Within days the event had come to be known as the Peterloo Massacre, an ironic echo of the victory over Napoleon at Waterloo four years earlier. The response of a nervous government was to praise the Yeomanry for their actions and to introduce a further string of repressive measures. Later that year, William Cobbett tried to travel to Manchester with the bones of Tom Paine (author of what some saw as the subversive book, *The Rights of Man*). The authorities prevented him, fearful that a few reformist bones could spark insurrection. The beginnings of reform (such as the Reform Act of 1832) were still more than a decade away.

THE PLUG PLOT RIOTS

The Chartist movement for electoral reform was a national campaign, but it found fertile ground in Manchester. In 1838 a huge meeting of Chartist supporters took place on Kersal Moor. Although nothing violent took place, some of the vocabulary of the protesters ('Be ready to nourish the tree of liberty with the blood of tyrants' being one of their slogans) reinforced the fears of those opposed to reform. The Chartists were behind the Plug Plot Riots of 1842 that centred on Manchester but affected much of Cheshire and Lancashire (so called because they involved halting production by pulling the plugs from the steam engines that powered the factories). Mobs of workers from the surrounding towns swept into Manchester, closing down the factories as they went and demanding the electoral reforms of the Charter and 'a fair

day's pay for a fair day's work'. They attacked the gas works in Gould Street and a nearby police station. By the time they reached Granby Row the crowd was estimated at between 10,000 and 15,000, and it took militia, backed up with field guns, and every available member of the town's police to disperse them. There were further Chartist riots in 1848, the year in which established governments across Europe were being overthrown and in which Karl Marx (working with Engels in Manchester) published his *Communist Manifesto*. Once again, the troops had to be employed in Manchester to restore order.

FENIANS

The Irish Republican Brotherhood were an illegal anti-British republican secret society, promoting armed rebellion against the British forces 'occupying' Ireland. On 11 September 1867 two of its members, Colonel Thomas Kelly and Captain Timothy Deasy, were arrested. A week later, they were being taken from the courts to the County Gaol on Hyde Road, West Gorton. The authorities were taking no chances with these dangerous prisoners – they were handcuffed in separate compartments of a locked police van, escorted by a dozen mounted police. As they passed under a railway bridge, about thirty armed men brought them to a halt and set about trying to open the van door with a sledgehammer and crowbar. Inside the van, Sergeant Brett ignored cries for them to open up and tried to look through the keyhole to see what was going on outside. His timing was particularly unfortunate, in that one of the rescuers chose that precise moment to fire a shot through the keyhole, killing Brett instantly. The van was eventually opened and the two prisoners escaped, never to be recaptured. However, several of their rescuers were captured and on 23 November three of them – William Allen, Michael Larkin and William O'Brien – were hanged. They had shouted 'God save Ireland!' in the dock as they were sentenced and, to those who sympathised with their cause, they became known as the Manchester Martyrs.

This was by no means the end of Manchester's troubles over the Irish question. In April 1921, in a night of violence, Republicans tried to set fire to a number of buildings in the city. They were pursued back to the Irish Club in Erskine Street, Hulme, where a gun battle took place; one of the Republicans was killed and another wounded, along with three police injuries. In the morning of 16 January 1939, three IRA bombs were detonated in Manchester; in one of these explosions, a fish porter named Albert Ross was hurled high into the air, landing on a passing postman. The postman was relatively unscathed but Ross died of his injuries. In 1992, sixty-four people were injured by two bombs, one near the cathedral and the other in a tax office off Bridge Street.

But June 15 1996 saw their most spectacular act of terrorism. A truck full of explosives was parked between Marks & Spencer and the Arndale Centre. Fortunately, sufficient warning was given for the police to clear the area completely so that no one was hurt when a huge explosion ripped through the city centre. The damage was widespread; windows were broken for half a mile around and estimates of the cost of repairs were put at anything up to £1,000,000,000.

VOTES FOR WOMEN!

The campaign for female suffrage began in 1832, after the Reform Act of that year failed to give them the vote. There was a concerted campaign led by John Stuart Mill in the run-up to the 1867 Reform Act, but this was again unsuccessful. In 1870 the National Society for Women's Suffrage held a meeting which was attended by the twelve-year-old Mancunian, Emmeline Goulden, the daughter of a Liberal calico-printing manufacturer. She would later marry the Socialist barrister and MP Richard Pankhurst. However, she did not get actively involved in the campaign for female suffrage until after the death of her husband. In 1903, she and her daughters Christabel and Sylvia formed the Women's Social and Political Union at their home in Rusholme.

They were struck by the way a violent demonstration by Manchester's unemployed in 1905 had forced the government into reforms, whereas decades of asking politely for the vote had got them nowhere. They set out to be more militant and attention-seeking and they succeeded, so much so that by January 1906 the *Daily Mail* had coined the abusive term 'suffragettes' for them – a title that they adopted as their own. If the suffragettes' campaigns were sometimes violent, their treatment by the police was even more so. Force feeding hunger-striking suffragettes via a tube inserted into the stomach via the nose was a particularly painful process.

The headquarters of the organisation soon moved to London, but suffragette activity continued in Manchester. Paintings in the City Art Gallery were vandalised, and a bomb attack on the cactus house in Alexandra Park in 1913 was blamed on them. Come the First World War and the Suffragettes changed from militant protesters to militant prosecutors of the war. They finally got their first recognition in the 1918 Representation of the Peoples Act, when women over thirty got the vote, but it would be 1928 before they were given the vote on an equal basis to men.

The General Strike of 1926 gave further scope for disorder on the streets, when a lorry driven by student blacklegs was turned over and set on fire by supporters of the strike.

GANG CULTURE

In recent years, Moss Side has been the part of the city most associated with gangs and their violent activities, but parts of nineteenth-century Manchester had an equally unsavoury reputation. In 1890, Manchester's most feared gang were the Bengal Tigers, named after the road in Harpurhey in which they lived. There is an account of a pitched battle (they called them 'scuttles') they fought in August of that year with a rival gang in Ancoats. They fought with knives, broken bottles and heavy leather belts with buckles so weighty that they could fracture skulls. They fought over many pretexts – religion, territory, women – and the female gang members were as prone to violence as their males. For more than three decades, these scuttlers terrorised parts of Manchester, but a number of factors are thought to have accounted for their decline – the long-term imprisonment of some of their ringleaders, slum clearance, which dispersed gang members, and the creation of more wholesome outlets for their energies, such as boys' clubs, street football and the cinema.

5

ON THIS DAY

1 January 1872: C.P. Scott took over as editor of the *Manchester Guardian*, a post he held until 1929.

1 January 1894: Manchester Ship Canal opened for traffic – Queen Victoria's official opening would follow in May.

1 January 1910: The aircraft company A.V. Roe and Co. was first registered at premises in Great Ancoats Street.

1 January 1930: Barton aerodrome opened for business as Manchester's airport.

9 January 1941: Maiden flight of the Avro Manchester Mark III – soon to be better known as the Lancaster bomber.

10 January 1949: The last of the old trams was taken out of service.

13 January 1840: Construction began on the first (temporary) Free Trade Hall, on the site of the later halls.

16 January 1939: IRA bombs exploded in Manchester.

17 January 1863: David Lloyd George, future prime minister, born at New York Place, Chorlton-on-Medlock.

30 January 1982: Belle Vue closed for the last time.

6 February 1958: Munich Air Disaster. Seven (later to be eight) Manchester United players, three club officials and eight journalists killed.

10 March 1817: The Blanketeers set off on their protest march to London.

15 March 1906: Rolls-Royce was registered at Somerset House (as a company based in Manchester).

23 March 1759: Parliamentary approval was given for the Bridgewater Canal.

29 March 1853: Queen Victoria conferred the title of 'City' on Manchester.

30 March 1819: John Edward Taylor acquitted of criminal libel – the start of events that would lead to the founding of the *Manchester Guardian.*

30 March 1825: The Mechanics' Institute, the first outside London, opened (initially in Cooper Street).

1 April 1904: The first Royce car – forerunner of the Rolls-Royce – made its initial appearance on the streets of Manchester.

2 April 1929: Manchester's temporary airport at Wythenshawe opened for business.

17 April 1888: The Football League first met in Manchester and founded the first professional league. This was the North's answer to the southern Football Association, and sought a more organised and professional approach to the sport. At first, no southern teams were invited to join because they were either not considered good enough or were too set in their ways.

22 April 1961: The New Manchester Hippodrome in Ardwick closed for the last time.

26 April 1877: Alliott Verdon Roe, Manchester aviation pioneer, born.

28 April 1910: Louis Paulhan lands in Burnage at the end of his historic flight from London.

1 May 1919: The first paying airline passengers landed in Manchester.

3 May 1956: First broadcasts from Manchester by Granada television.

4 May 1904: Mr Rolls met Mr Royce at the Midland Hotel and a motoring legend was born.

5 May 1821: The first edition of the *Manchester Guardian* published.

5 May 1969: Central and Exchange stations were closed to passengers under the Beeching cuts.

12 May 1785: James Sadler made the first ever manned hydrogen balloon ascent from Manchester, taking off from a garden in Long Millgate.

16 May 1896: Chorlton Recreation Ground, a gift to the people of Manchester from Lord Egerton, opened.

17 May 1966: Near riot at the Free Trade Hall, as Bob Dylan played his notorious 'Judas' concert with an electric backing group. Later released as a bootleg under the (erroneous) title of *Live at the Albert Hall*.

26 May 1766: The Manchester Lunatic Hospital admitted its first patient.

31 May 1845: John Owens issued instructions that would lead to the founding of Owen's College (later to become the University of Manchester).

1 June 1941: Heavy bombing of Manchester, the Assize Courts being among the buildings destroyed.

2 June 1841: Vicious battle in Stevenson Square between Chartist supporters and the Anti-Corn Law League. The Anti-Corn Law League won, having hired a team of Irish thugs.

2–6 June 1868: First meeting of the Trades Union Congress at the Mechanics' Institute.

7 June 1757: The start of food shortages that would lead to the rioting known as the Shudehill Fight in November 1757.

8 June 1908: Roe's prototype flying machine took to the air for the first time – the beginning of Avro aviation.

14 June 1919: Mancunian John Alcock and adopted Mancunian Arthur Whitten Brown took off on their historic first non-stop crossing of the Atlantic by aeroplane.

16 June 1946: The first post-war international airline service from Manchester left Ringway for Paris.

21 June 1948: 'Baby' – also known as the Small Scale Experimental Machine and the world's first stored program computer – ran for the first time at the University of Manchester.

23 June 1896: Trafford Park estate sold by the de Trafford family to Ernest Hooley, who would begin its development.

24 June 1752: Manchester Infirmary opened for business in Garden Street, Shudehill.

25 June 1868: Strangeways prison officially opened.

25 June 1938: Ringway airport officially opened by Air Minister, Sir Kingsley Wood.

27 June 1882: Daniel Adamson holds a meeting of Manchester's great and good at his house, at which the idea of the Manchester Ship Canal was first put forward.

4 July 1887: The Bridgewater Canal Company was bought by the Ship Canal Company for £1,710,000 – at that time, the largest cheque ever written.

6 July 1909: King Edward VII opened the new Manchester Royal Infirmary buildings at Oxford Road.

13 July 1905: Manchester Docks opened by King Edward VII.

15 July 1785: The first mail coach service to Manchester was inaugurated.

17 July 1761: Opening of the Bridgewater Canal, Britain's first artificial waterway linking Manchester to the coalfields at Worsley.

17 July 1934: King George V opened the Central Reference Library.

18 July 1904: The Ardwick Empire (later known as the New Manchester Hippodrome) opened.

27 July 1752: The Manchester Infirmary (later Royal Infirmary) received its first patient – one John Boardman (twenty-two) suffering from scrofula.

3 August 1893: Manchester's mayor granted the status of Lord Mayor.

13 August 1964: The last hanging in the UK took place at Strangeways prison.

16 August 1819: The Peterloo Massacre.

22 August 1985: Fifty-four holidaymakers died in an air disaster at Ringway airport.

24 August 1959: The *Guardian* dropped the name *Manchester* from its title.

26 August 1906: Final service in St Peter's Church before its demolition, leading to the creation of St Peter's Square.

28 August 1914: The first four Manchester Pals' battalions of the First World War were formed.

1 September 1940: Start of the evacuation of 72,000 children and 23,000 adults from Manchester, as the Second World War broke out.

1 September 1908: The last patients (except for one very sick one) were decanted from the old infirmary in Piccadilly and into the new one on Oxford Road.

2 September 1852: The opening of Manchester's first public library.

8 September 1957: Pauldens department store gutted by fire – many died.

10 September 1641: Edward Barlow, local Catholic martyr, later to become St Ambrose Barlow, hanged, drawn and quartered at Lancaster.

11 September 1977: Closure of Belle Vue amusement park.

13 September 1877: Official opening of Manchester Town Hall.

15 September 1830: The Liverpool & Manchester Railway, the world's first modern railway, officially opened.

20–22 September 1227: Manchester granted a right in perpetuity to hold a fair on these dates by King Henry III.

24 September 1838: First meeting of the Anti-Corn Law Association at the York Hotel, King Street.

25 September 1642: The start of the Civil War battle for control of Manchester.

1 October 1823: The founding of the Manchester (later Royal Manchester) Institution, that would lead to the building of what is now the City Art Gallery.

2 October 1642: Parliamentary forces celebrated victory in the Civil War battle for the town.

3 October 1885: Public holiday in Manchester as parliamentary approval for the Ship Canal was announced.

6 October 1829: The start of the Rainhill trials, at which the steam locomotive came of age.

6 October 1899: Rylands Library opened (on Mrs Rylands' wedding anniversary – public access was not given until the start of the new century).

7 October 1873: The new Owen's College buildings opened for the first time.

8 October 1921: King George V opened the new Royal Exchange.

13 October 1905: Birth of the suffragette movement, when Christabel Pankhurst and Annie Kenney disrupted a Liberal party meeting at the Free Trade Hall, at which Winston Churchill was speaking.

14 October 1902: Prime Minister Arthur Balfour opened the Manchester School of Technology (later UMIST).

23 October 1922: The first international air flights from Manchester, serving London and Amsterdam, with onward links to Berlin.

23 October 1838: The charter incorporating the townships of Manchester, Cheetham, Hulme, Ardwick, Chorlton-on-Medlock and Beswick as a borough was granted.

26 October 1868: The foundation stone for Manchester Town Hall was laid.

7 November 1963: Manchester's horse racing course finally closed.

11 November 1887: Lord Egerton cut the first sod of the Manchester Ship Canal.

25 November 1934: Riot at the Free Trade Hall, as the British Union of Fascists held a meeting under the banner 'Fascism Explained! Hear how fascism will save your country and your job!'

28 November 1745: The vanguard of Bonnie Prince Charlie, the Young Pretender's, forces arrived in Manchester, en route (as they thought) to London and the overthrow of King George II.

30 November 1998: Prince Edward re-opened the Royal Exchange, after the IRA bomb damage had been repaired.

1 December 1902: Much of the city switches from horse-drawn to electric trams.

2 December 1771: Manchester's first bank, the 'Manchester Bank' of Messrs Byrom, Allen, Sedgewick and Place, opened at Bank Street, St Ann's Square.

3 December 1908: Premiere of Elgar's *Symphony No. 1, in A flat major* at the Free Trade Hall, conducted by Dr Hans Richter.

4 December 1875: Manchester Town Hall topped out.

9 December 1960: The first episode of the soap opera *Coronation Street* was broadcast.

14 December 1838: Manchester's first municipal election.

16 December 1838: The first meeting of Manchester Borough Council.

16 December 1856: The Halle Orchestra gave its first concert at the Free Trade Hall.

21 December 1804: Rochdale Canal opened.

22 December 1940: Manchester's worst air raid of the Second World War.

24 December 1944: V1 flying bombs attacked Manchester.

26 December 1912: Opening of the Opera House, Quay Street.

31 December 1968: Royal Exchange closed as a trading concern.

6

SOME LANDMARK MANCHESTER BUILDINGS

Manchester is a more interesting city to walk over than London. One can scarcely walk about Manchester without coming across examples of the grand in architecture. There has been nothing to equal it since the building of Venice.

Building News, 1861

Making any selection of buildings from a city as rich in its architectural heritage as Manchester is fraught with danger. Readers will inevitably disagree with whatever choice I make, so it may be as well to explain my selection criteria at the outset. First, I make no claim that these are necessarily the dozen or so architecturally best buildings in Manchester, or even that they are the best examples of their kind, although many will be held in high regard by the citizens of Manchester. Some are iconic landmarks that immediately say 'Manchester' to anyone who knows the city, but mostly they are chosen because they tell an important part of the city's story. They are not listed in any order of preference or merit, but are in roughly chronological order.

MANCHESTER CATHEDRAL

Manchester Cathedral (or the Church of St Mary, as it started life) pre-dates the Domesday Book, which includes a reference to it. It was thought that the original church was located somewhere in the vicinity of St Ann's Square and dated from the seventh century. This building was thought to have been destroyed in a tenth-century Danish raid, and a new place of worship was built, roughly on the site of the present one. The present church, which is in the Perpendicular Gothic style, has origins going back to 1215. During restoration work in 1870, the authorities were excited to find what appeared to be a small piece of Saxon stonework – the Angel Stone – in among the foundations. It bears the words (in Old English) 'Into thy hands O Lord I commend my spirit'. However, while some date this stone to the eighth century, other research suggests that it may actually date from the eleventh or twelfth centuries.

The oldest surviving parts of the present building are the piers supporting the tower, which date from around 1380, but much of the rest has been greatly remodelled, restored, added to or altered over the years. The earliest addition was the St Nicholas chantry, endowed by the Gresley family some time before 1311. One of the most important features of the interior is the finely-carved medieval woodwork (in particular, the choir stalls and misericords), dating from 1485 to 1506, and said to be among the finest in Europe. The Victorian era was particularly active on the restoration front, with major works being carried out in 1815, 1850–70, 1868 and 1897. During this period, all the exterior stonework of the cathedral was replaced and the tower heightened, giving it the appearance of a nineteenth-century building.

In terms of the church's status, it was made a Collegiate Church in 1421/22, giving it a responsibility for ministering to an area of some 60^2 miles. At the same time, the new Lord of the Manor, Thomas la Warre, set up a college of clergy associated with the church. At this time, the church was one of the few sources of educated men to help administer the country. Among their other duties was that of praying for the souls of the men killed on the king's military campaigns in France. St Marys was made a cathedral in 1847, and in 1952 became a Grade I listed building.

The cathedral suffered serious damage during the bombing raid of December 1940. Virtually the last bomb of the raid struck the cathedral's north-east corner, lifting the entire lead roof off and dropping it back, miraculously, in place. The Lady Chapel, the Ely Chapel (the latter dating back to 1515) and much of the Regimental Chapel were destroyed, and the High Altar lay under 10ft of rubble. But, within twenty-four hours, a fund had been opened and craftsmen were lining up to help with the restoration. However, this restoration was not completed until 1960 and, from 1975 onwards, they set about replacing the west windows with stained glass – just in time for the IRA bomb of 1996.

THE OLD WELLINGTON INN AND THE SHAMBLES SQUARE

One of the most prominent (and certainly the most travelled) reminders of Manchester's medieval and Tudor past, the Shambles, was traditionally the area of a town occupied by butchers. An inn is thought to have stood on or near to the original site of the Old Wellington Inn since the fourteenth century. The third floor of the building is a seventeenth-century addition to the 1552 original structure. The inn, the only surviving Tudor building in the city centre, became a public house in 1830 (originally known as the Vintner's Arms, later the Kenyon Arms, or Kenyon's Vaults). Prior to that, in 1692, it was the birthplace of John Byrom, a member of a prominent local family, the author of hymn 'Christians Awake' and the inventor of a system of shorthand. His family ran a drapery business from the premises. It had acquired its present name by 1865, at which time just the ground floor was given over to licensed premises and the upper storeys were let to a variety of businesses, including (at various times) a maker of scientific instruments and a fishing tackle shop.

Sinclairs Oyster Bar which adjoins it is relatively new, the building dating from 1738. It was at one time the venue for one of Manchester's earliest gentlemen's clubs and, for some fifty-eight years, was run by an ex-soldier named John Shaw. He was a stickler for order and any reveller dawdling after closing time was liable to be sent on his way home with the help of a bucket of cold water. Only after his death in 1796 was it re-named Sinclairs, and oysters were added to the menu (and the name) after 1845.

The two buildings survived the wartime bombing and were raised by 4ft 9in during the redevelopment of the area in the early 1970s. The IRA bomb put paid to the new development that surrounded them in 1996 and created an opportunity to dismantle and move the buildings some 300 metres across Cateaton Street to a more appropriate setting, nearer the cathedral, where they re-opened for business in late 1999.

The third side of the new Shambles Square is occupied by the Mitre Hotel. When first built in 1815 it was known as the Old Church Tavern, and it only acquired its present name in 1835. It is said that Bonnie Prince Charlie reviewed his troops outside the earlier building which stood on the site, in 1745.

ST ANN'S CHURCH

The late seventeenth and early eighteenth centuries were a period of considerable religious dissent, both within Manchester and nationally. In 1685 the strongly Catholic James, Duke of York, succeeded to the throne as James II. Tories broadly supported this and upheld the doctrine of the divine right of kings, while the Whigs were more pro-parliament and opposed his succession. James was driven out in (what is slightly misleadingly named as) the Bloodless Revolution of 1688, in which his daughter and son-in-law William of Orange and Mary were invited in by sectors of the British establishment to overthrow him. Thereafter, those who supported the return of the Stuarts were known as Jacobites.

Within Manchester, the differences were reflected in the churches. The Collegiate Church was strongly Tory and supported the Stuart dynasty, while the Whigs attended the Cross Street Chapel and opposed the Jacobites. They had their own pubs (the Bulls Head Inn for the Tories and the Angel Inn for the Whigs) and even had rival dancing groups, respectively sporting the Stuart tartan and orange blossom motifs.

Lord of the Manor Sir Edward Mosley had a daughter, Lady Ann Bland, who took particular exception to the pro-Jacobite sermons delivered in the Collegiate Church and decided to provide an alternative venue, one that was more supportive of the new dynasty. In 1708 she secured an Act of Parliament for the construction of what became St Ann's Church in St Ann's Square (provided she left enough space unenclosed to allow the town's longstanding fair to continue to be held there). It was consecrated in 1712 and opened just in time for, in 1715, a Jacobite mob burned down the Cross Street Chapel (the other alternative to the Collegiate Church). It was later rebuilt, with the help of a £1,000 grant from parliament and, meanwhile, St Ann's Square and surrounding area by the 1750s became the town's most fashionable residential area.

The church is thought to be the work of Derbyshire architect John Barker, though his original design has been much altered over the years, including by Town Hall architect Alfred Waterhouse. Joseph, writing in 1816, details some of these alterations:

> It formerly had a cupola, in some degree corresponding with the rest of the building, but which, being in bad repair and deemed dangerous by surveyors, was taken down in 1777, and a spire erected, by subscription, in its place. The new spire, in the opinion of the neighbouring inhabitants, was, at least, as much to be dreaded as the old cupola, and was soon afterwards taken down.

Built originally of local Collyhurst sandstone, the church has been patched up over the years with a variety of other sandstones from different areas, which do not quite match and give it something of a patchwork appearance.

The church survived the IRA bomb of 1996, which blew most of its windows out and caused £125,000 of damage, just as it had completed a major refurbishment programme.

THE OLD MILL, REDHILL STREET

The development of the steam engine liberated manufacturers from the need to be next to a fast-flowing watercourse to power their machinery, and made the development of Manchester as a major manufacturing centre possible. In 1782 the town had just two cotton mills in and around the area. Within a decade, this increased to fifty-two. Richard Arkwright built a steam-powered mill in Miller Street, Shudehill, in 1782. It was destroyed in 1940. However, the steam engine was only used to pump water for a waterwheel; it fell to Peter Drinkwater, who became the mill-owner in 1790, to use steam directly to power cotton machinery for the first time, and it increased the capacity of his Piccadilly Mill at Auburn Street by a factor of thirty.

These early mills suffered from a tendency to catch fire whether from straightforward accidents, resulting from the hazardous use of oil or gas lighting in an environment thick with inflammable cotton waste, or through deliberate sabotage by irate handloom weavers, was not always clear.

Today, the oldest surviving mill in Manchester is the Old Mill on Redhill Street (formerly Union Street), Ancoats, opened by the Murray Brothers in 1798. This six-storey building is one of a series of imposing structures backing onto an arm of the Rochdale Canal. The canal itself was new at the time, having only received parliamentary approval in 1794 – in fact, the mill pre-dated the cross-Pennine link the canal was designed to provide – which did not open until 1804. At their peak, the Murray brothers alone employed 1,300 workers in this and the adjoining mills they owned. The manufacturing mills tended to differ from those used purely for storage, in that they had the largest possible windows to help light the spinning operations. The mills tended to be of load-bearing brickwork on the outside, with a (relatively) fireproof internal construction of cast-iron columns supporting the iron beams that carried the floorboards.

The area's importance has been recognised by a government proposal for it to become a World Heritage Site (a proposal not, to date, taken up by UNESCO).

MERCHANTS' WAREHOUSE, CASTLEFIELD

We have seen elsewhere the importance of the canals in supplying the residential and business needs of a growing town. The Bridgewater Canal was opened to Manchester in 1761 and a hub of commercial activity began to develop around its terminus at Castlefield, where Manchester had its Roman origins. Brindley's first warehouse was opened in 1770 and by 1829 the commercial area stretched from the canal to Deansgate. Merchant's Warehouse, dating from 1827–8, is the earliest of these to survive. These buildings were some of the architectural wonders of their day. A German architect, Karl Schinkel, visiting Manchester in 1825, marvelled that 'The enormous factory buildings are seven to eight storeys high … where three years ago there were only meadows'. He added that they were already so black with soot that they looked as if they had been there for 100 years. A particular feature of the warehouse is its 'shipping holes', allowing barges to enter for direct loading or unloading.

The canal basin reminds us of two important facts about Manchester. The first is the economic importance of the canals. Among other things, their ability to bring coal to Manchester far more cheaply than before made steam power a financially viable option, without which the early development of the town would not have been possible. The second, more uneasy, reminder is of the extent to which the prosperity of early Victorian Manchester was built (albeit indirectly) on the slave trade. Britain abolished the slave trade in 1807, but did not end its practice in its colonies until 1838. The southern states of America did not abolish it until after the Civil War, in 1865. So, much of the goods that were traded through this warehouse in the early years – like cotton and sugar – would have been the products of slavery.

During the American Civil War, the blockade of southern ports by the Unionist side led to supplies of cotton to Manchester being cut off, resulting in the Cotton Famine of 1862–3. Despite the great hardship that this caused to those employed in the textile industry, most Mancunians never wavered in their support for Abraham Lincoln and the abolitionist cause, earning them the heartfelt gratitude of the American President. A statue to Lincoln stands in Brazennose Street.

Little is known about the history of the Merchants' Warehouse. Other warehouses, far better documented, were demolished, many of them in the 1960s. It was known to have taken in goods from both the Bridgewater and Rochdale Canals, and that it was damaged by the Luftwaffe in 1941 and partially gutted by fire in 1971. Only its robust construction saved it from being completely lost, and it stood for a time in a derelict and dangerous state. Today it is used for offices and studios, following its restoration in 1995–7.

LIVERPOOL ROAD STATION

Manchester's Liverpool Road shares with Liverpool Lime Street the distinction of being the world's first railway stations. But Manchester nearly did not get a station at all. The railway was, as we see elsewhere in the book, conceived first and foremost as a freight carrier – passengers (and the infrastructure they require, such as stations) were very much a secondary consideration for the promoters. Moreover, the railway, as originally approved by parliament, did not even come into Manchester, stopping short near the New Bailey prison in Salford. There was a good deal of opposition to 'any locomotive engine moved by steam-air' within Manchester;

people feared that they would run amok, like crazed beasts, and the choice of a Salford terminus may in part have been a tactical one, to get around rooted opposition from landowners in the part of Manchester preferred as a terminus.

It was only through a second Act of Parliament, secured in May 1829, that George Stephenson was able to bridge the Irwell and build a 2-mile extension into Manchester. Even then its route was tightly circumscribed and the line had to be enclosed by an iron fence. (Restrictions were even tighter at the Liverpool end – for many years, trains were hauled out of Lime Street by a stationary steam engine and only connected to a locomotive at Edge Hill.)

The choice of Liverpool Road reflects the promoters' view of the railway as primarily a freight carrier; the location was not particularly central to Manchester for passengers, but the promoters saw it as vital that they were near the warehousing area used by the canal companies. In practice, the railway soon developed its own warehousing area, totalling some $4,000,000\text{ft}^2$ by 1837. The terminus was in fact considered so far out for passengers that a separate ticket office had to be opened in the town centre, at 57 Market Street. From 1831 there was even an omnibus service (free to first-class passengers) connecting the town centre ticket office and the platform – or at least it connected to where the platform should have been for, until 1834, the station had neither platform nor weather protection. The facilities, when they were provided, included separate entrances and ticket offices for first- and second-class passengers. First-class passengers also had the dubious benefit of a sundial (not, perhaps, the ideal timepiece for somewhere with a climate like Manchester's, but reflecting the fact that railways at this time still worked on local, not standard 'railway' time). Between Manchester and Liverpool there were no recognisable stations, just places where the trains habitually stopped.

This disjointed arrangement would not survive for long. In 1842, permission was given for a new, much larger, more

central station at Hunts Bank (later renamed Victoria). This was a joint venture by the Liverpool & Manchester and Manchester & Leeds railways and was in its day the largest station in England. Passenger services were relocated from Liverpool Road to Hunts Bank in 1844. The railway buildings at Liverpool Road were sold to the former Greater Manchester County Council for £1 in 1978. Today, they form part of the Greater Manchester Museum of Science and Industry.

ST MARY'S, 'THE HIDDEN GEM', MULBERRY STREET

The present building, buried away on the back streets off Albert Square, replaced one dating from 1794 – the first Catholic church built since the Reformation in any major English centre of population (the Relief Act that allowed Catholics to develop places of worship was only passed in 1791 and work on the original church began a year later). Prior to that, from 1774 Catholics from a wide area used to worship at the Rock Street Chapel, which stood at the junction of Fountain Street and West Mosley Street.

The present church's principal features are an unusual spire, based on a medieval German design, and its elaborate interior decoration, with life-sized statuary. It was its interior that caused Catholic Bishop of Salford, Herbert Vaughan, to coin the building's nickname, when he said in 1872, 'No matter what side of the church you look, you behold a hidden gem.' Not everyone shared his admiration of the church's eclectic styling. The eminent Victorian architectural critic Augustus Welby Pugin (not known for holding back on his criticisms of others' buildings) said of it, 'It shows to what depths of error even good men fall when they abandon the true thing and go whoring after strange styles.'

Another cleric, the Revd Arthur J. Dobbs, gives this account of the church's changing catchment:

> The Roman Catholic Church sought to tackle Manchester's deepest troubled area, which lay in between Deansgate and Albert Square. A church was built in 1794 in Mulberry Street on a site crowded in by intensive low quality housing on land which so recently had been open meadow and grazing pasture. St Mary's much rebuilt, still stands on the same plot of land, now surrounded by the edifices of sophisticated materialism, which is probably more spiritually barren ground than the vileness of the eighteenth century.

The rebuild followed the collapse of the roof of the original church in 1835, as repairs to it were being carried out by incompetent builders. Attempts at that time to relocate the church proved unsuccessful and it had to be rebuilt in situ. Today it reminds us of the staggering contrast between the beauty of the church and the squalor of its early surroundings – of how the two can co-exist in a city, and of the impact that the contrast must have had for its parishioners. The church was much restored in 1993–4 and the following year added a series of paintings showing the 'Stations of the Cross' by Norman Adams (RA) to its decoration.

WATTS' WAREHOUSE, PORTLAND STREET

John Watts started out as a farmer from Didsbury, who opened a draper's shop called the Bazaar on Deansgate in 1796. The first lines he sold were ginghams, handwoven by his wife and six sons. The business grew, and his brothers Samuel and James joined him in it. By 1836 his focus was more on the wholesale side of the business and three of his other employees – Thomas Kendal, James Milne and Adam Faulkner – bought out the retail business, which would later become Kendal Milne. Watts moved first to Brown Street and, by 1855, his brothers were able to commission the S&J Watts warehouse on Portland Street. John Watts was by this time truly one of the great and the good – Prince Albert, no less, stayed with him at his home in Abney Hall, Cheadle, when he came to Manchester in 1857 to open the Art Treasures Exhibition.

In its day, the building was by a long margin the largest in Manchester (standing 100ft high, 300ft long and 90ft deep). It was also one of the most expensive, and arguably the most elaborately decorated, business premises. It is said to

be modelled on a Venetian palazzo, the Fondaco dei Turchi. Each floor is in a different style – there is a rusticated Italianate ground floor and, above it, Elizabethan, back to Italianate, then French Renaissance, Italianate again, topped out by a frieze and, at either end and above the entrance bays, towers with rose windows in the French Gothic style – what Parkinson-Bailey calls 'a veritable cathedral of commerce' and which architectural historian Niklaus Pevsner said, 'Aptly encapsulates the spirit of self-confidence mixed with a touch of brashness.' Some found it difficult to believe such a grand building had been provided merely for the storage of textiles – this from the *Freelancer* magazine in 1867:

> I am not naturally of a sceptical or suspicious cast of mind. I have eaten sausages and kidney pudding without asking questions but when I was told that this was only a warehouse I felt it was necessary to draw the line of credulity somewhere.

By contrast, the rear elevation, not visited by customers, was finished in plain brick. Inside, an elaborate wrought-iron staircase led the customers to floors where 600 staff sold goods from a sales list 384 pages long.

Like many of Manchester's historic buildings, it had something of a chequered existence in the twentieth century. It was hit with incendiary bombs during one of the big wartime raids. Members of staff, posted as firewatchers, struggled to put the fires out, but all seemed lost when their water supply was cut off. However, they somehow managed to extinguish the flames by smothering them with textiles. The Watts company lasted until 1960, when it was taken over; by 1969 it had become part of the Courtaulds group, and in 1972 the building was threatened with demolition.

The building stands as a reminder of Manchester's transformation from primarily a manufacturing town to the centre for the distribution of the products of the region's cotton industry. The town had had something of a role as a distribution centre for the cotton industry from as long ago as the 1500s, but by the 1840s it was the centre for some 280 cotton towns and villages in the region. At its peak, around 65 per cent of the world's trade in cotton goods passed through Manchester – something approaching a billion tonnes a year – and Watts were Manchester's single largest wholesale drapery. Since 1982, the building has been used as a hotel.

MANCHESTER TOWN HALL

Manchester's current Town Hall is not the first of its kind. A timber and plaster building is mentioned in records dating from 1473. It was known variously as the Boothes and the Court House (since the Court Leet – the medieval body primarily responsible for the administration of the town – met there). The open lower storey of the building would have been used by stallholders on market days. It fell into disrepair over the years and would have been demolished as part of the street improvements of 1776, if not before.

For a time, the administration of the town was conducted from the police office in King Street until, in 1825, a new Town Hall was opened at the junction of King Street and Cross Street. This building was not without controversy, since it involved the demolition of the house previously occupied by Dr White – a local medical man of some renown – and early conservationists were none too happy about it going. However, the town got an imposing new building in the then highly-fashionable Greek Revival style, with a portico modelled on the Erechtheion in Athens. Its designer, Francis Goodwin, was a pupil of the famous architect John Soane. The building cost the town the not-inconsiderable sum of £39,547, but had a relatively short life in its original use before its replacement was commissioned. It went on to serve as the town's lending library and as a bank, until it was demolished in 1912. However, the portico was saved and re-erected beside the lake in Heaton Park, where it can be seen to this day.

The cost of the old Town Hall would pale in comparison to the new one, and 1867 – when the city was still recovering from the crippling economic effects of the cotton famine of the American Civil War years – was an odd time for the city fathers to commission what would become the world's costliest building. A two-stage competition was launched, which attracted 137 entries. The outcome was again controversial.

The eventual winner, Alfred Waterhouse, only came fourth on architectural merit; many favoured the more romantic entry by local architect Thomas Worthington, described by the *Manchester Examiner* as a 'Rhineland vision'. However, Waterhouse's scheme was considered superior in terms of lighting, ventilation and ease of access, and he was allowed – rather unfairly, some thought – to add some of Worthington's best features to his scheme retrospectively. These included a 281ft-high clock tower that made it, until 1962, Manchester's tallest building. Thus Manchester got what Waterhouse described as a building that was thirteenth century in spirit but 'Essentially of the nineteenth century and adapted to the wants of the present day'.

The building was officially opened on 13 September 1877. Among the attendees were the Lord Mayor and council, the Lord Chief Justice of England and a crowd of 66,000. One notable absentee was Queen Victoria – some say her absence was because she was still in deep mourning for Prince Albert, others that she disapproved of the city's radical mayor, Abel Heywood (who had once campaigned for a republican Britain), and the local Liberal politicians, some of whom had recently approved the erection of a statue to the well-known arch republican Oliver Cromwell outside the cathedral (now to be found at Wythenshawe Park). Republicans or not, the councillors had been desperate to get Queen Victoria along to the opening. They even asked the artist Ford Madox Brown to omit any reference to the Peterloo Massacre in his mural for the Great Hall of the Town Hall, lest this (for some reason) offended the monarch.

The original budget of £500,000 had to be roughly doubled and the statistics for the scheme (350 rooms, 700 external windows, 14 million bricks and 500,000ft^3 of stone) help to explain why. The building survived both the Blitz and 1945 development plans to replace it with a hideous piece of contemporary architecture. In February 1952 it became a Grade I listed building and stands today as the city's greatest monument to Victorian civic pride. It is also much in demand as a film set, where it doubles, among other things, as the interior to the Houses of Parliament; this, despite A.J.P. Taylor's description of it being 'in a rigid Gothic which looks as though it had been bought by the yard'.

UNIVERSITY OF MANCHESTER MAIN BUILDING, OXFORD ROAD

As long ago as 1640, Manchester lobbied the Long Parliament for the establishment of a northern university, but the decision went in favour of Durham, rather than Manchester. When Manchester's time came, the university was originally named Owens College after its original benefactor, the wealthy merchant John Owens. In 1846 he left £96,000 in his will to found a college for the instruction of young men 'in such branches of learning and science as are now and may hereafter be taught in the English universities'. It was to be strictly non-sectarian (a departure from the practice in other higher education institutions of the day) and it was to be open to everyone 'without respect to place of birth, and without distinction of rank or condition in society'.

It was based originally in Richard Cobden's old house, at the corner of Quay Street and Byrom Street. After a shaky start, the introduction in 1859 of examinations from the University of London led to a boom in student numbers – and a new campus was needed.

A site on Oxford Road was found by October 1868, by which time £77,000 had been subscribed to the project (though the final cost would escalate to nearly £180,000). Alfred Waterhouse was appointed as the architect and the foundation stone was laid in September 1870. The building contained all the accommodation the fledgling university needed – lecture rooms and laboratories (including what was then the most up-to-date chemistry laboratory in the country), examination rooms, administration, a medical school and even a geological museum. When the new college opened in 1873, it could offer any degree available from the University of London, with tuition fees of just 10*s* 6*d* for a full course of lectures.

The new body was the subject of vicious attacks from the educational establishment of the day, who organised a campaign against it getting university status in its own right. *The Times*, in 1877, expressed the view that giving university status to Manchester would undercut the important social distinction of a degree, and the *Saturday Review* concluded that 'Anyone educated in Manchester would certainly be dull and probably vicious'. There were also doubts as to whether a smoky place like Manchester could confer the keen corporate feeling with which students to Oxford or Cambridge were blessed. It took until 1884 for the university to get even limited degree-awarding status, and until 1903 before it became a university in its own right. A century later, the university merged with the city's Institute of Science and Technology. Today, the combined university can claim more Nobel Prize Laureates than any other British university, other than Oxford and Cambridge, and in 2009 was ranked the eighth best university in Europe and twenty-sixth in the world.

BARTON ARCADE

Designed by Corbett, Raby & Sawyer, this was one of the first buildings to be erected on the newly-widened Deansgate. The light and elegant three-storey iron and glass arcade was mass-produced in MacFarlane's Saracen Foundry in Glasgow. The foundry's proprietor, Walter MacFarlane, started his career as a silversmith, which may help explain the quality of some of the detailing. The building has an Italianate flavour; some say it shows the influence of the Galleria Vittorio Emanuele in Milan, though others question this. It was extensively restored in the 1980s.

ROYAL EXCHANGE

The Cotton Exchange lay at the heart of Manchester's central role for the industry but there had been earlier exchanges. The second one was nearly destroyed in an 1812 riot, protesting at the Borough Reeve's decision to allow a lunch to be held for the supporters of the repressive politicians Castlereagh and Addington. The rioters finally did for it three years later, in a riot over the price of potatoes. The old exchange had been extended in 1836 and 1845, and had been given the title Royal when the Queen visited it in 1851. By 1874, it was decided that new premises were required and the site which had at one time been the offices of the Anti-Corn Law League was acquired to that end. Up to 8,000 traders would assemble and conduct their business in a quiet setting that was in marked contrast to the frenetic noise of other market floors. Around the largest of the room's three domes ran a quotation from the Book of Proverbs: 'A good name is more to be chosen than great riches, and loving favour rather than silver and gold'.

The building of the Ship Canal led to a dramatic increase in the number of traders using the Exchange, and work began on a further extension to the building in 1914, giving a site area of 1.7 acres and a trading floor roughly twice the size of the present one – said to have been the largest trading room in the country. It was delayed by the First World War and was finally opened by King George V in 1921, just as the cotton industry was entering its period of terminal decline. By 1926 trade with India was less than half of its 1913 level, and with China less than a third. The potential consequences for Manchester were huge. As Sir William Himbury of the British Cotton Growing Association put it in 1929:

If the cotton trade ceased to exist tomorrow Great Britain would become a third-rate power, from a commercial point-of-view, and probably one fourth of the population would have to emigrate, as it would no longer be possible for them to earn a living in this country.

The decline continued throughout the recession of the 1930s and the Second World War years. By 1958, imports of cotton goods exceeded exports for the first time, and an industry that had once employed 1,100,000 people across the country had virtually ceased to exist. When the Exchange finally closed in 1968, there were only fifteen cotton mills left in business in the area.

OLDHAM ROAD TENEMENTS

Manchester was one of the first local authorities to recognise its responsibility for doing something about the appalling housing conditions it had inherited from earlier, unregulated, times. The 1844 Manchester Borough Police Act was the first of its kind, and effectively made it impossible to develop back-to-back housing within the then boundaries of the town (Leeds, for example, did not have similar powers until the 1930s). A further act in 1853 prohibited cellar dwellings, and in 1867 Manchester got powers to close unfit dwellings without compensation and bring in rudimentary Building Regulations, some eight years before they became a national requirement.

The city's other big slum clearer was the railway – their goods yards, stations and track swallowed up acres of inner city housing. The new goods station at London Road (Piccadilly) alone required the demolition of some 600 houses, and the building of Central station in the 1870s displaced some 1,200 people. In total, it is estimated that some 20,000 Mancunians may have been displaced by the railways alone.

The problem was that neither the council nor the railway companies saw it as part of their job to replace the houses they demolished. The displaced families simply moved on to the next slum area, making the overcrowding problem there worse. Manchester's Medical Officer of Health was a solitary voice calling for public bodies to provide decent, affordable housing for the poor. According to his 1884 report:

> If helping the poor in this way – doing for them what they cannot do for themselves, or aiding them to do what they cannot accomplish alone – be socialism or communism, the more we have of it the better, when wisely and judiciously administered.

But he was up against not just accusations of communism and socialism, but also the feeling that the suffering of the poor was inevitable and, indeed, God-given. It took an initiative by the Bishop of Manchester, in helping to set up the Manchester and Salford Working Men's Dwellings Company in 1881 – after they had converted a mill and built a new tenement block in Holt Town, the council responded in kind. In 1889 the council announced plans to build a five-storey tenement building, fronting onto the Oldham Road. They employed an architect named Henry Spalding, who had built similar buildings for the London County Council. Mr Spalding was no dewy-eyed idealist – he knew of the practices of some slum tenants, of stripping any spare timber out of their homes for firewood and stealing any lead pipework for scrap, and he consequently specified concrete skirting boards and iron pipework. As for the other sanitary arrangements:

> I do not wish to underrate the importance of hygiene, but hygiene is not valued by the working man and so for its advantages he does not care to pay ... Some years ago it was the custom to provide baths in many of the dwellings; now it is seldom done ... Also, it is no great hardship for people of this class to share a scullery with another family; they have for the most part been used to it for most of their lives.
> (Henry Spalding, 'Block Dwellings', *Journal of the Royal Institute of British Architects 1900* – page 254)

The building was, and is, austere in the extreme – only the Oldham Road frontage had anything in the way of ornamental detailing (presumably so as not to offend the sensibilities of any passing suburban commuters). Most of the dwellings consisted of just two rooms and shared a kitchen and water closet with a neighbour. There were also communal laundries and drying rooms. But, however inadequate these provisions may be by modern standards, they were still too costly for some Ancoats slum dwellers, many of whom were employed (if at all) on a casual basis. Many of those displaced by redevelopment would still have no option but to move to the next slum area. Even so, this development at least marked the beginning of the council taking responsibility for the provision of social housing – something that would play so large a part in the activities of the council in the century that followed.

RYLANDS LIBRARY

John Rylands was the biggest cotton manufacturer in the country, employing some 15,000 people. He was a devoutly religious man and a benefactor to many of the towns in which he had business interests. Stretford, where he lived, got a Town Hall, a library, baths, a coffee house and contributions towards orphanages and homes for the elderly. He died in 1888 and his widow, Enriqueta, set in motion plans to create a public library in his memory to house his collection of rare and ancient books (for this reason some have referred to it as the Taj Mahal of the North-West). She commissioned Basil Champneys, the architect of the library at Mansfield College, Oxford, to build it on a site at Deansgate. No expense was spared on the building, from the 4ft 6in of concrete foundation covering the entire site, to the 6in concrete roof, chosen to avoid the fire risk of anything wooden. Only the finest materials and craftsmen were used and Mrs Rylands oversaw every minute detail of the construction, frequently falling out with (and overruling) the architect. She even secured agreements with neighbouring landowners to limit the height of any future redevelopment, so that her library should not be overshadowed.

Despite its Gothic appearance it was a very modern building for its day – steel-framed, one of the first public buildings in the city to be lit by electricity as a cleaner alternative to gas (they generated their own electricity supply, an arrangement that continued until 1950) and with what was (for its time) quite sophisticated air conditioning to counter the pollution of a Victorian industrial city.

Equally lavish was Enriqueta's stocking of the library; she augmented her husband's collection with that of the Earl Spencer at Althorp (at a cost of £210,000) and the Crawford collection (£155,000) and the library boasts one of the earliest examples of a New Testament text, illuminated medieval manuscripts, a fine Gutenberg Bible, the second largest collection of William Caxton's printed works, not to mention the personal papers of John Wesley, John Dalton and Elizabeth Gaskell. In total the building and its contents cost her £1 million. It was opened in October 1899 and Mrs Rylands was given the freedom of the city. After her death in 1908, her will endowed the library with further private collections and £200,000 to buy more books. In 1921, the library opened

its doors to local families who wished to deposit their family papers for safekeeping (in the days before county records offices for Lancashire or Cheshire existed).

It was later merged with the University Library, to form the third largest academic library in the country. More generally, it stands as one reminder of the way in which rich benefactors could contribute to the life of a community, in the days before public finances were seen as the first source of funding.

MIDLAND HOTEL

The Midland Railway was a relative latecomer to Manchester. Their Manchester terminus, in Central station, did not open until 1880, half a century after the town's first railway was opened. Nonetheless, the station, closely modelled on London's St Pancras, is a grand design in the Victorian manner, with its 210ft-wide single-span roof (the third largest in the country). The original intention had been to attach the hotel serving the station directly onto the front of it (again, in imitation of the arrangement at the London terminus, with its St Pancras Hotel) but this for some reason did not materialise and the station was left with a rather unimposing frontage that was only originally intended to be temporary. Instead, they compromised on a covered walkway between the station and the rear of the hotel, an arrangement that lasted until just after the Second World War.

The design of the hotel was entrusted to their in-house architect Charles Trubshaw and opened in 1903. A.J.P. Taylor (as we have already seen, no fan of Manchester's architectural heritage) speaks of its 'grandiose tastelessness' and Biddle describes it as 'Vast, ostentatious and pompous in red brick with copious orange-brown terracotta decoration, including pepper pot corner turrets.' But it was in its day the last word in luxury, with 400 bedrooms, four restaurants, electric lifts, a winter garden, an 800-seat theatre (to replace the Lane's Gentlemen's Concert Hall – demolished to make way for the hotel) and an early form of air conditioning. It was also structurally advanced, being another early example of steel-framed construction.

Anyone important visiting Manchester has tended to stay or dine there. Customers have included prime ministers (messrs Blair, Brown and Cameron among the more recent ones), entertainers (from Tom Jones and the Spice Girls to Luciano Pavarotti – the Beatles were thrown out of the restaurant for being improperly dressed) and royalty (including the Queen Mother, Prince Edward and the Beckhams). Hitler was said to have coveted the building as a regional headquarters for his Nazis after they invaded, and Mr Rolls famously met Mr Royce there, to found the motor car company that bears their names. Mrs Horniman founded England's first repertory theatre company in the hotel theatre. They staged smoking concerts there, but women could only attend if accompanied by a man, and young men (however these were defined) had to have permission to attend from their employer. Its original purpose, as a railway hotel, ceased to be in May 1969 when Central station closed. It was not until the spring of 1986 that the station was re-born as the G-Mex Exhibition Centre.

CENTRAL LIBRARY

Manchester can boast what was probably the world's free public library. In 1654 a wealthy businessman, Humphrey Chetham, endowed the library, along with a bluecoat orphanage. Aston described the library thus in 1816:

> He also left one thousand pounds 'for or towards a library, within the town of Manchester, for the use of scholars, and all others, well affected, to resort unto' ... He further directed that the books should remain there forever 'as a public library', and that 'care should be taken that none of the books should be taken out of the library at any time' and that they should be 'fixed or chained as well as may be' for their preservation.

As we saw, among the later users of Chetham's Library were Karl Marx and Friedrich Engels, who used to meet there while Marx was writing his *Communist Manifesto*.

Manchester had a proliferation of libraries by the early nineteenth century. The Manchester Circulating Library, based in the Old Exchange in King Street, had been going since 1757, and by 1815 had a stock of almost 10,000 volumes for its 370 subscribers. The Portico opened in 1806 in Mosley Street and offered a library and reading room. Its first secretary was a doctor at Manchester Infirmary who would become better known as the author of a work of reference – Doctor Peter Mark Roget (he of the thesaurus). There was also the Manchester New Circulating Library in Broom Street and a variety of other lending libraries, promoted either by worthy institutions like churches or rather more down-market commercial organisations offering the literary novelties of the day.

It was not until 1850 that parliament gave local authorities powers to establish public libraries. An act of that year gave them the power to spend the product of a halfpenny rate on the building, fixtures and fittings of a library (though, curiously, not on books). Not everyone in Manchester was enthusiastic about the new powers. To some, books were all very well if the common people were limited to reading the scriptures or Adam Smith's *Wealth of Nations* – volumes that would reinforce the established order. But they were equally liable to use their new-found literacy to study dangerous revolutionary works, such as Tom Paine's *Rights of Man* or the Chartist newspaper *Black Dwarf*.

Fortunately, there was enough support for it within Manchester to ensure that the town would become the first to open a new library under these powers. Businessmen at the Exchange raised over £4,300 towards it and Prince Albert donated eighteen volumes, specifying that they should be freely accessible to all classes without distinction. At the other end of the social scale, 22,000 working men clubbed together to raise £800 towards the project. 25,000 volumes were assembled, and the library that was opened in September 1852 was revolutionary in its scope. It offered a reference library, free to all, and a lending library, open to anyone who could find two burgesses of Manchester or Salford to act as guarantors for the return of the books.

The opening ceremony featured many of the literary giants of the age – Charles Dickens, William Thackeray and Sir Edward Bulwer-Lytton – as well as the Earl of Shaftesbury and John Bright MP (notwithstanding the fact that the latter had opposed giving local authorities these powers in parliament). It was hailed by the Chartists as the dawn of a socialist paradise. The library was a great success, making 138,000 loans in the first year to the one in six of Manchester's population who could read at that time. Suburban branches were soon opened and, during the Cotton Famine of the 1860s, the reading rooms also became popular places for starving cotton-workers to keep warm. The original library building at Campfield became unsafe and the library was moved into the old Town Hall. This in its turn was declared unsafe and closed in 1911 and, for over twenty years, the library had to operate out of cramped temporary premises in Piccadilly. Eventually, a competition was held in 1926 which would eventually give rise to the current Central Reference Library.

It was designed by the London architect E. Vincent Harris (who was also responsible for the adjoining Town Hall extension) and the foundation stone was laid by Prime Minister Ramsay MacDonald in 1930. By the time King George V opened it in July 1934 it had cost £410,000 to build and equip (over and above the £187,797 site cost). It has room for over a million volumes on its shelves and its main hall can seat over 300 readers, making it the largest reading room in Britain (other than the old British Library reading room). In its day, it was the world's largest municipal library and was referred to as the 'British Museum of the north'. (A.J.P. Taylor, once again, dismisses it as 'an exact model of an iced wedding cake on a gigantic scale that would win an honourable mention in a contest for the most hideous library in existence'). St Peter's Square, over which it looks, was the former site of St Peter's Church. The Square was created by the corporation in 1907 and some 2,500 Mancunians are buried in the crypt beneath the tram stop there.

AND SOME MODERN TURKEYS!

Architect Alfred Waterhouse's works (the Town Hall, the university main building, the Refuge building and the (sadly-bombed) Assize Courts) were a major adornment to the architecture of the town. Contrast this with the work of the architectural practice Wilson and Womersley, which gave us not only the disastrous Hulme Crescents but also the unloved tiled façades of the Arndale Centre, often described as the biggest public toilet in Europe. Another development unlikely to appear on any sentient being's list of most-loved Manchester buildings is the Piccadilly Plaza, which so comprehensively blights one side of the Piccadilly Gardens. Yet, when it was opened in 1965, everybody seemed to admire it. Naturally, architects loved it – the *Architectural Review* said it was 'Good in its architectural details and good to walk around,' but Manchester Corporation called it 'A most exciting development' and the *Evening Chronicle* cooed that it was 'A wonder of the new age'. It makes one wonder what on earth our descendants will be admiring in fifty years' time.

7

WHY IS IT CALLED THAT?

Manchester: How did Manchester get its name? Tradition had it that the Roman version of it was *Mancunium*, from which we get the modern name for its inhabitants – Mancunians. But scholars have also suggested other variations for the Roman name – *Manutio, Mammium, Mamucio* or *Mamucium* (which could derive from a Celtic word for a breast-shaped hill, describing the outcrop on which the original settlement stood). Aston, writing in 1819, offers us a British name – *Mancenion*, meaning 'a place of tents', and for good measure throws in the possibility of *Manduesedum*. Between the sixth and tenth centuries, references are found to *Mameceastre, Manceastre* and *Mameceaster*. The Domesday Book refers to *Mamecestre*, as does the Charter granted to the town in 1227 by Henry III, while a 1322 survey of the Manor has it as *Mamcestre*. By the time of Henry VIII, they would appear to have settled on the modern name, according to legislation affecting the town passed during his reign; however, one wonders whether the wording has been 'tidied up' by subsequent historians, since Leland's *Itinerary*, dating from about the same time (1540) still uses *Mamcestre* and *Manchestre*.

So that's all perfectly clear! Now for some other familiar Manchester names.

Ancoats: Originally from *ana cots*, meaning 'old cottages'. By the early thirteenth century it had become *Elnecot* and there are fourteenth-century records of somebody called Henry de Ancotes bequeathing land there.

Ardwick: Thought to be a combination of an abbreviation of the name (King) Aethelred into *Ard*, and *wic*, a farm or small hamlet. Earliest records from 1282 have it as *Atherdwic*. In Tudor times, it was alleged to be a village which had problems with 'wild women, disorderly houses, children playing giddy gaddy and too many dunghills in the road'. The Green there was originally a private garden, serving local residents. It was acquired by the corporation in 1867.

Aytoun Street: Probably from Roger Aytoun, the spendthrift young husband of the much older Lady of the Manor, Lady Barbara Minshull. He sold off a lot of her land in Chorlton-on-Medlock for development from the 1790s.

Baguley: Possibly from the Cheshire Baguley family, or something related to a badger clearing. Sir William de Baguley owned parts of south Manchester in 1319 and it remained in the family's ownership until the seventeenth century. Sir William married one of King Edward I's illegitimate daughters

Barlow Moor: Named after the Barlow family, who owned large parts of the area from the early thirteenth century to 1785, and who lived in Barlow Hall. One of their number, Edward Barlow, was ordained as a Catholic priest in France in 1617 and made the dangerous decision to return to England to follow his vocation. He was arrested and executed for his faith in 1641, and was made a Saint (St Ambrose Barlow) in 1970.

Belle Vue: When John Jennison first opened his leisure attraction he called it the Strawberry Gardens, but business-man George Gill persuaded him to relocate to a site between Stockport Road and Hyde Road, with greater potential for expansion. The previous owner of the site had operated low-key leisure activities from the site under the name the Belle Vue Tea Gardens.

Beswick: In the tenth century it was known as *Beaces hlaw*. *Hlaw* is Anglo-Saxon for a natural hill used as a burial mound. By around 1200 it was known as *Beaces wic*.

Blackley: The name is thought to have originated from the Anglo-Saxon *Blaechleah*, meaning 'a dark wood or dark clearing'. The area formed part of the Manor of Mamecestre, granted in 1086 to Albert de Grelley, one of the families that travelled to England with the Conqueror. The name may have been reference to a clearing rather than a wood, since the area appears (from records of 1215) to have contained a royal deer park. By 1360 there was a religious establishment in the area, and the present Victorian church is built alongside the site of the old chapel.

Bradford: The settlement is recorded in 1196 as *Brade ford* or broad ford – probably a lost crossing of the River Medlock. Medieval Bradford is said to have boasted water meadows, woodlands full of roe deer and honey bees, hawks, herons, eagles and, up to about the year 1400, wolves.

Brooklands: In 1856, a Manchester banker and businessman, Samuel Brooks, bought land in this area from the Earl of Stamford, to develop as an up-market suburb, so Brooklands is built on Brooks' land.

Burnage: There is a reference dating from 1320 to *Bronadge*, or 'Brown hedge' – a possible reference to the brown stone walls, or 'hedges' used to separate fields in this area.

The area has fifteen other alternative spellings of its name. More recently (1906–12) it became the site of Manchester's first garden village, to provide decent homes for working people, with 'light and air and pleasantness of outlook', not to mention amenities such as hot and cold water, bathrooms and electricity.

Cheetham Hill: A very desirable residential suburb in the early nineteenth century. An area known as Cheetwood Village lay within it. For part of its history, land in the area was owned by the Chetham family, though whether this has anything to do with the origin of the name is not certain, since the earliest reference to it goes back to the year 1212. An alternative explanation is that it means 'village by a forest or wood'.

Chorlton-cum-Hardy: There are various options for the derivation of this name. One was that it is from the Old English words *Ceorlatun-cum-ard-ea*, meaning 'a settlement of *ceorls* (Saxon freemen) by trees near the river'. But some early maps show Hardy as a separate settlement next to Chorlton, leading some to believe that the name refers to *Coerlfrith's tun* (or settlement) at *Hearda's* island. Yet another suggestion was that the names Chorlton and Hardy were only combined when it became necessary to differentiate the area from Chorlton-on-Medlock.

Chorlton-on-Medlock: Records of the area go back as far as 1202, when the tenant was listed as one Gospatrick de Chorlton (from whom it conceivably took its name). An alternative suggestion is that it means 'village of the free peasants on or by the Medlock'. However, the development of the area appears to have been a largely nineteenth-century phenomenon, since its population at the first 1801 Census was just 675 (by 1851 it had risen to 35,558). It became part of Manchester in 1838. It changed its name from Chorlton Row to Chorlton-on-Medlock as part of a review of local government in 1832.

Clayton: Possibly a *tun* (village) on clay soil, or associated with the Clayton family, longstanding owners of much of the area. The present Clayton Hall was built in the sixteenth century and stands on the site of an earlier moated building. It was acquired by the corporation in 1893. Even earlier, in the twelfth century, the area was owned by the Byron family. Legend has it that Sir Hugo Byron went off to the third Crusade, leaving his lovely young bride behind. Time passed, Sir Hugo failed to return and word filtered back that he had been killed. Shortly afterwards, his wife died of a broken heart. As it happened, Sir Hugo had only been delayed, and actually met her funeral cortege on his homeward journey. He promptly renounced his knighthood, gave up warfare and became a monk.

Collyhurst: The name means 'wooded hill' and the fact that the hill consisted largely of red sandstone gave the area its alternative name – Red Bank. Most of the Roman and medieval stone building that went on in Manchester used stone from this area. There also seems to have been coal mining, since the area was known from 1322 to have been made grimy by coal dust.

Crumpsall: Named from Old English words meaning 'a crooked piece of land beside a river'. It refers to the fact that the original village of Crumpsall Green lay on an oxbow bend in the River Irk and was frequently flooded and difficult to farm. It is another area with alternative versions to its name – *Curmisale* (1282), *Curmeshalle* or *Curmeshal* (1320), *Curmesale* (1404) and *Cromshall* (1548).

John Dalton Street: Named after the eminent scientist John Dalton, who lived and worked in Manchester for many years and from 1817 to 1844 was the President of the Manchester Literary and Philosophical Society.

Didsbury: In medieval times Didsbury was part of a much larger feudal estate centred on Withington. The name is thought to derive from the Anglo-Saxon *Dyddy's burg* – a township in the ownership of someone called Dyddy.

It stood on a low cliff near a place where the River Mersey could be forded. Thirteenth century records variously have it as *Dydesbyre*, *Dydesbiri*, *Dodesbury* or *Didsbury*. The local church, St James, was established in 1235 and became a parochial chapel in 1352, when a burial ground for plague victims was developed there.

Egerton Road: Egerton was the family name of the Dukes of Bridgewater.

Fallowfield: The area was known from the fourteenth century as *Fellafeld*, and one of its early owners was named Jordan de Fellafield. The name is thought to mean 'fallow or yellowish land'.

-gate: places with names ending in gate (like Deansgate, Greengate and Milgate) tend to be of Danish origin (*gat* being their word for a road). The Dean part of Deansgate is thought to have come from a lost river, the Dene, so it is a road that runs by a river.

Gorton: Folklore has it that the area is named after the blood (or gore) that flowed in an early battle between Saxons and Danes in the area. In fact the name means 'dirty town' or 'dirty farmstead'. A watercourse called the Gore Brook still flows through the area and its water looks filthy. This is due not to pollution, but to local deposits of peat or iron ore that colour the water. The earliest reference to the area goes back to 1282.

Hanging Bridge: Probably from *Hen* (Old English for wild birds or fowl) and *Gan* (situated between two hills).

Harpurhey: In the early fourteenth century a man called William Harpour enclosed an area of 80 acres that had previously formed part of the forest of Blackley. *Haeg* was an old word for an enclosed area, giving us Harpour's *haeg*. Harpour was evidently given the land in or around 1327 by Sir John la Warre, the Lord of Manchester.

Hulme or -hulme: Places with names ending in the suffix -hulme tend to have been Danish settlements in their early days. It comes from a Danish word for a small island surrounded by water or marshland. Hulme itself is surrounded on three sides by the Rivers Irwell and Medlock and by the Cornbrook. The suggestion is that the Danes occupied the area some time between the Roman and Norman invasions. There are also suggestions that there was Roman settlement in the area, but the evidence has so far been elusive.

Irk: The river's name may come from *Iwrek* or *Irke*, thought itself to have originated from the word for Roebuck, signifying that it was once a fast-flowing river.

Irwell: The name of the river is something of a mystery, but may derive from the Anglo-Saxon *ere well,* meaning 'hore or white spring'.

Kendal, Milne & Co.: In 1796 a farmer from Didsbury, John Watts, opened a draper's shop in Deansgate. The business grew and diversified, and among the new staff he recruited in 1830/1 were Thomas Kendal from Westmoreland, who had previously worked as a draper's assistant in London, James Milne from Swinton and Adam Faulkner of Flixton. By 1836, these three were able to buy out Watts, who went on to develop the wholesale side of his drapery business, eventually building the grand S&J Watts warehouse on Portland Street. The other three traded as Kendal, Milne & Faulkner, but Faulkner died, aged just fifty, in 1862, whereupon the business became the familiar Kendal, Milne & Co.

Ladybarn: In the thirteenth century, rights over large parts of what is now south Manchester were granted to a body called the Abbey of Our Lady. They collected tithes of corn which were stored in a building called Our Lady's Barn, which in turn gave its name to the surrounding area.

Levenshulme: An area with multiple possible spellings of its name. In 1246 there was *de Lyweneshulm*, which translates from Old English and Old Scandinavian as 'the island of a man named Leofwine'. In 1322 there was a choice of *Levensholme* or *Lywneshulme*, or there was *Lewenesholm* (1361), *Leysholme* (1556), *Lensholme* (1758), *Lensom* (1587) or *Lentsholme* (1635).

Longsight: The usual explanation offered for the derivation of this name is wrong. It is alleged that Bonnie Prince Charlie, when approaching Manchester from the south in 1745 and, arriving in Longsight, said 'It seems a long sight to Manchester'. The trouble was that the area was known to have been called Longsight well before the Prince set foot in it. Some suggest the name derives from *Long-shut*, meaning a shallow, low-lying area, or from the long and short sights of a gun that was once kept at the Waggon and Horses public house. Looking even further back into history, it was referred to as Grindlow Marsh. Another possibility was that it was thought of as a sub-division of Gorton, rather than a settlement in its own right.

Medlock: The river's name may come from the old English *medlacu, medlac* or *medelac* – meadow stream.

Mersey: The name of the river derives from *Maeres ea*, meaning the border river, since it traditionally marked the border between the Kingdoms of Mercia and Northumbria.

Miles Platting: Does not appear as a separate entity on maps until the 1820s. One suggestion for the derivation of its name is that it derives from *Platt,* a small area of land, and *Miles,* a corruption of mills, suggesting mills tightly packed together.

Mosley Street: The Mosley family were long-standing Lords of the Manor of Manchester. Nicholas Mosley was Manchester-born but rose to be Lord Mayor of London and Sir Nicholas. He bought the manorial rights for £3,500 in 1596 and his descendant, Sir Oswald, sold them back to the Corporation of Manchester for £200,000 in 1846.

Moston: Means the town on the moss and, though there is an early reference to Sir Ralph de Moston having property interests there, it seems likely that he took his name from the area, rather than vice versa.

Newton Heath: Not surprisingly, the name describes 'a new town on the heath'. Somewhere called Newton appears on local records as far back as 1322.

Northenden: The settlement appears in the Domesday Book and its name is thought to come from the Anglo-Saxon *norp worpign* – or 'north enclosure'. An alternative explanation is that it means 'northern dale or valley' – a reference to its proximity to the Mersey. In medieval times there was an important ford of the River Mersey at Northenden – important because there was no bridge between Sale and Stockport to carry trade on the Salt Road between Cheshire and Manchester. The ford was unusual, in that the northern and southern parts of it were not opposite to each other – travellers had to go about 500ft up or downstream. Could the northern dale be a reference to the northern part of the crossing?

Oldham Street: Named not after the place but after an eighteenth-century felt-maker and associate of John Wesley, Adam Oldham. It was first opened to the public in 1772.

Openshaw: First referred to in 1282 as an open woodland where the King and local nobles hunted deer and wild boar.

Oxford Street/Oxford Road: Work on Oxford Street in Chorlton-on-Medlock began in 1792. It was designed to link St Peter's Square with the Wilmslow turnpike. It needed to be built on an embankment, to lift it above the floodplain of the Medlock, and the material needed for this was excavated from the adjoining area that came to be known as Little Ireland. This area was notorious for its grinding poverty, poor housing and disease (not least because it was unsurprisingly low-lying and next to the filthy river Medlock).

Palatine Road: A road linking the two counties palatine of Cheshire and Lancashire. They were areas once governed by courts palatine, in which a duke or an earl has powers to rule independent of any interference from the monarch.

Philips Park, Bradford: Named after Mark Philips, elected as Member of Parliament for Manchester in 1832, who both contributed to and campaigned for the park, which was part-government funded under legislation passed in 1840. Opened in 1846, it was one of the first of its kind in the country.

Platt Fields: Part of an estate originally owned by a family called Platt.

Rusholme: Another area that has very variable spelling, appearing as *Russum* in 1235, *Russhum* in 1420, *Rysshulme* in 1551 and *Risholme* in 1568. One suggestion is that the name derives from the Old English *ryscum*, meaning 'at the rushes'. A watercourse known as the Rushbrook once ran across it. A large part of it was owned by Henry de Rusholme in the thirteenth century, though which took their name from the other is a matter for speculation.

Sharston: Possibly named after Sharston Hall (built 1701, probably on the site of an older house – demolished in 1986).

Shudehill: The earliest recorded reference to it was in 1554, though the name is thought to go back much further. There is some speculation that its name derives from the word *shude*, meaning the husks of oats, though why this should be so is not immediately clear.

Strangeways: Before the area was developed, there were Strangeways Park and Gardens, which previously occupied the area. The area is referred to in a manorial survey of 1322. It was owned by a family named Hartley in the seventeenth century and had passed to the Earl of Ducie by 1850, by which time only part of the estate remained intact. The hall was demolished in 1860, and the architect Alfred Waterhouse began work on the prison shortly thereafter. It opened in 1868. The Assize Courts were also built there.

Stretford: From the Anglo-Saxon *straet* (street) and *ford* (crossing place), a reference to a crossing of the Mersey at Crossford Bridge.

Tib Street: Traditionally the pet-shop quarter of the city centre, it takes its name from the now largely lost River Tib, which flowed into the Medlock. According to some accounts, it was barely more than a ditch.

Trafford Park: The de Trafford family moved into the area south-west of modern Manchester city centre in 1017. At some time between 1672 and 1720 they moved to a new family home, at the north-western end of what is now Trafford Park Road. The house was then called Whittleswick Hall, but they renamed it Trafford Hall and the area is thought to derive its name from this family, who retained their interest in it until 1896.

Whalley Range: The area used to be known as Jackson's Moss. It was developed as 'A desirable estate for gentlemen and their families' by Victorian banker and businessman Samuel Brooks. He was born near a place called Whalley in Lancashire and named his own home Whalley House, so Whalley Range probably has the same origin. The Salford-born actress Joanne Whalley took her stage name from Whalley Range.

Whitworth Street: Named after the pioneering mechanical engineer Joseph Whitworth, inventor of many things, from a standard screw thread to the mechanical street sweeper.

Withington: Appears as *Widign-tun* in Domesday book, at which time it appears to have been little more than a wasteland. One suggestion is that this Anglo-Saxon name comes from words meaning 'a settlement or farmstead near a willow wood'. Another suggestion is that a Saxon chief named

Widdingas lived in the area and gave his name to it. By the early thirteenth century it was an independent sub-manor of Manchester, held by William, son of Wulfrith de Withington.

Wythenshawe: Part of Cheshire until 1931, the name is thought to derive from the Old English words for 'withy tree' and 'wood'. The estate was for many centuries controlled by the Tatton family of Wythenshawe Hall. The hall itself dates from about 1540, but is on the site of an older building.

AND SOME LOST NAMES

Alport town: Hundreds of slum dwellers in this area were evicted – without compensation – in order to build the Castlefield viaducts that carried the Bridgewater Canal into Manchester. The construction of the Great Northern Railway Goods Warehouse in 1896–8 completed the obliteration of this community.

Gotherswick: A hamlet near to Manchester, recorded in 1320, but since absorbed into Harpurhey.

Nuthurst: A separate medieval community now swallowed up by Moston, but remembered by a road and a park bearing its name.

8

THOSE MAGNIFICENT MEN ... FLYING OUT OF MANCHESTER

The city has a long association with the development of flight. Here we look at some of the key stages in that association.

UP, UP AND AWAY ...

The dawn of manned flight took place on 21 November 1783, when Monsieur Pilatre de Rozier and the Marquis d'Arlandes took to the air in their hot air balloon above the streets of Paris, following smaller-scale experiments by the Montgolfier brothers. Within days, an alternative technology made its debut; a Parisian scientist, Jacques Charles, flew the first man-carrying hydrogen-filled balloon. Word of this did not take long to reach Manchester, and in December 1783, a gas-filled balloon released from the grounds of the Manchester Infirmary made a 45-mile flight to Cromford in the Peak District. However, this was not manned, and it would be 1785 before the first intrepid aviator looked down on the Manchester rooftops.

In the meantime, the launching of hot air balloons had become such a hobby among less responsible Mancunians that they became a fire hazard to crops and wooden buildings. The Boroughreeve and Constables issued an order on 29 October 1784 banning them, along with 'squibs, crackers and rockets'.

Britain entered the era of flight in October 1784 when James Sadler, son of a pastrycook, flew over Oxford in his hydrogen balloon, and it was he who brought his balloon to Manchester the following March. This was very much a money-making exercise; the balloon was exhibited in the Exchange prior to being flown, with visitors being asked to part with 1*s* for the privilege (or 6*d* for 'working people and servants'). Those wishing to see it actually flying would be charged between 5*s* and half a guinea. Five thousand people assembled on 12 May to witness the spectacle, though how many of them watched it for free from outside the reserved area is not clear.

The flight took place from the garden of a house in Long Millgate, later the Manchester Arms Hotel, near what is now Victoria Station. The street name Balloon Street commemorates the flight. The crowd saw the start of a flight that lasted an hour and three-quarters and deposited Sadler safely between Blacow Bridge and Radcliffe. A repeat flight the following week was less successful. Atmospheric conditions carried him up to an altitude of 13,000ft, freezing him before depositing him rather forcefully at Pontefract and taking him on a cross-country drag, ending near Gainsborough. To make matters worse, members of the public who recovered his balloon helped themselves to its silk fabric.

It would be 1812 before Manchester saw another balloon flight; again it was Sadler on board, and this time the elements deposited him 6 miles east of Sheffield. From the 1820s, balloon ascents became a popular feature of fairs and other celebrations in Manchester and elsewhere. Sadler's son William took up the family business, flying (among others) from the site of what later became Salford's Victoria bus station. His career came to a violent end when he collided fatally with a factory chimney near Oswaldtwistle in September 1824. Among the most frequent flyers were George and Charles Green, who took paying passengers on tethered flights to allow more people the experience of being airborne (at 5s a time). Green also gave Mancunians their first sight of a parachute, dropping a live chicken in a basket. The no-doubt surprised fowl landed safely in Silver Street.

A frequent venue for flights was the Vauxhall Pleasure Gardens, located in what was (in the early nineteenth century) an area noted for country air and pleasant scenery, between the Rochdale Road and the River Irk, at Collyhurst. Here, the Greens hit upon the idea of keeping the crowds informed of their progress by sending back homing pigeons at regular intervals. By the 1830s, town gas had replaced hydrogen as the fuel of choice, but there were sometimes problems with the quantity or quality of gas the local gasworks could provide. In the case of one flight, in 1836, the crowd waited until early evening for the balloon to inflate. They finally lost patience and started throwing fireworks and generally trying to set the balloon alight. Police had to be called to restore order.

In 1852, the first balloon ascent took place from the new public gardens at Belle Vue. This featured one Arthur Goulston (stage name Giuseppe Lunardini) and ended in tragedy. Taking off in bad weather against advice, Arthur/ Guiseppe attempted to leap from the balloon as it returned to earth, but got caught up in some ropes and was dragged along until he dashed his brains out on a stone wall. Another favoured venue for ballooning was the Pomona Gardens near Ordsall Hall, until its closure in 1888 to make way for the Manchester Docks.

The public gradually grew blasé about balloon ascents and operators looked for new novelties. These included a trapeze act, performed in fancy dress beneath the basket, and parachute jumps from the balloon (at least some of which were successful).

Manchester is also associated with a curious application of ballooning to journalism. During the Franco-Prussian war of 1870 the town of Metz was besieged, and the only war correspondent on the spot was George Robinson of the *Manchester Guardian*. He had no way of getting his despatches out, until he hit upon the idea of making small fabric balloons filled with coal gas and floating them over the enemy lines in the hope of someone picking them up and forwarding the attached messages to the newspaper. A number of these rather speculative messages actually reached the *Guardian* offices.

EARLY AVIATORS

Manchester had its share of (more or less eccentric) aviation pioneers. As early as 1693, a Rivington farmer and staunch Presbyterian, Moses Cocker, leapt from the roof of his barn, hoping to be borne aloft by a home-made pair of wings. He only survived thanks to the soft landing made possible by his manure heap.

Frederick D. Artingstall put his faith in the power of steam, driving a pair of flapping birdlike wings. His experiments started in the 1830s and, in 1866, he attached a model of his invention to the ceiling by string at his house in Collyhurst. The device jerked about convulsively, without flying, until the boiler exploded. Later experiments with a rotating wing device did actually generate some lift, until the wings fell off.

A Denton tailor named Moorhouse developed a large kite, capable of lifting the weight of a man into the air. He exhibited this successfully at Belle Vue Gardens in 1842, but perhaps wisely declined the opportunity of replacing the three 56lb weights it carried with himself.

ALLIOTT VERDON ROE

In April 1877 the wife of a Patricroft doctor gave birth to her fourth son, christened Alliott Verdon Roe (Verdon being the mother's maiden name). He disappointed the family, who had hoped he would follow in his father's professional footsteps, and became in turn a successful racing cyclist, an apprentice at the Lancashire & Yorkshire Railway works in Horwich and an engineering officer on ships plying between Britain and Africa. On board ship he became fascinated by the graceful gliding of the albatrosses that followed them, and they inspired him to build a number of model gliders. By 1902 he had left the merchant navy and was working as a draughtsman for the motorcar manufacturers Brothers-Crockett Ltd.

When he heard of the Wright brothers' pioneering flight he entered into correspondence with the brothers, and tried to awake the nation's interest in powered flight. His efforts were not met with success – the Engineering Editor of *The Times* responded to his letter with the view that all attempts at 'artificial aviation' were doomed to failure, and the *Manchester Guardian* said in an editorial of 11 September 1908, that, 'We cannot understand to what practical use a flying machine that is heavier than air can be put'. Undeterred, Roe decided in 1906 to devote himself full time to aviation. He became Secretary of the Aero Club, before travelling to America to assist a man named Davidson in experiments with a large steam-driven helicopter.

Returning to England, he entered one of his models in a competition organised by the *Daily Mail*. It beat over 200 competitors and, with the £75 prize money, Roe was finally able to build a full-sized prototype. He did so in a shed at the Brooklands motor racing circuit, where there was a prize of £2,500 on offer for the first person to fly round the circuit before the end of 1907. Roe at first lacked a sufficiently powerful engine to meet this deadline and it was not until June 1908 that his aircraft first flew.

Roe's fledgling enterprise led a hand-to-mouth existence in a variety of premises, until his brother provided him with a workshop in the basement of his Brownsfield Mill on Great Ancoats Street, and it was here that the company of A.V. Roe and Company was registered on 1 January 1910. His aircraft was due to fly at the second Blackpool Flying Meeting in July but, on the way there, sparks from the train that was carrying it set fire to it and destroyed it. Roe worked day and night to complete a second aircraft and was able to take to the air by August Bank Holiday, before a crowd in Blackpool. Despite the hastily-constructed plane crashing three times, Roe won a £75 consolation prize for his efforts.

By 1912 the company had moved to better premises at Clifton Street, Miles Platting, and the War Office had placed their first order with the company – for three biplanes for use at the Central Flying School. These were the forerunner of the aircraft that was to become the mainstay of flying training during the First World War. Roe did the initial designs for the Avro 504 early in 1913 and over 8,000 of them would eventually be built. They provided the foundation for one of Britain's major aircraft manufacturers.

THE 1910 LONDON TO MANCHESTER AIR RACE

In November 1906 Lord Northcliffe, the proprietor of the *Daily Mail*, offered a £10,000 prize to the first person to fly from within 5 miles of the paper's head office to within 5 miles of their Manchester office; no more than twenty-four hours, with just two stops along the route, would be allowed. At this time no Briton had even made a powered flight, and the longest hop seen anywhere in Europe (by Alberto Santos-Dumont) was barely 700ft. It was 1909, by which time Louis Blériot had flown the English Channel, before British aviation was sufficiently advanced even to contemplate the challenge. An early attempt by Samuel Franklin Cody, the first man to fly in Britain, met with failure and, by 1910, it turned into a race between English hopeful Claude Grahame-White and the Frenchman Louis Paulhan.

Grahame-White was a dashing young car dealer and racing motorist. He had only recently purchased his Farman monoplane and had just eighty minutes' flying experience with it, having previously taught himself to fly in a Blériot without taking a single lesson. His main motive in entering the race was to gain publicity for the flying school he intended to open. He departed on 23 April 1910 and got as far as his second landing place, in Lichfield. There, a gale-force wind overturned his craft, damaging it so badly that it had to be taken back to London for repairs. These were completed by 27 April but, by then, Paulhan had arrived in London and managed to take off an hour before Grahame-White. Paulhan had the unusual navigational aid of a special train, flying a white flag, guiding him to Manchester. Reporters on board the train scribbled messages about the progress of the race, that they threw out at stations for onward transmission to their editorial offices. The race was world-wide news, followed in cities from New York to Moscow.

Grahame-White was still 57 miles behind as darkness fell and they both landed. He made the risky decision to bridge the gap by flying at night and at 2.54 a.m. he took off by the light of car headlamps and was led towards Manchester by a steam-powered car. Paulhan got news of this at 4.00 a.m. and set off in pursuit. Grahame-White found himself facing ever-stronger headwinds until he was making virtually no progress and had to land, exhausted. The more experienced Paulhan managed to find slightly better conditions by climbing to over 1,000 feet, and at 5.25 a.m. landed at Manchester (ironically on the field at Fog Lane, Burnage, that his rival had earmarked for landing). Paulhan stepped from the plane a broken man, saying 'Never again – not for ten times £10,000.'

More than fifty years later, Paulhan would return to Manchester in rather greater comfort, as the guest of honour at the opening of the new terminal building at Manchester's Ringway airport. Nor did Grahame-White do badly from the publicity; he received a £105 consolation cup and was able to promote a hugely successful tour of the United States, which in turn enabled him to buy 220 acres of pasture at Hendon. This he turned into London's first airport, until it was acquired by the RAF in 1925, and is now the site of the RAF Museum.

FROM MANCHESTER – AND ACROSS THE ATLANTIC

The world took notice of the successful completion of the London to Manchester challenge. Even Orville Wright commented, saying that 'An aeroplane with sufficient gasoline capacity to attempt a Transatlantic flight can now be built.' In 1913, the *Daily Mail* offered another £10,000 prize for the first successful transatlantic flight. It would take a few more years and the hot-house of aviation development provided by the First World War before this prize would be claimed, but again the feat had a Manchester connection.

Around the time that Paulhan was completing his epic flight, the Empress Engineering Company on Stockport Road was taking on a new apprentice. The proprietor, Charles Fletcher, was a keen amateur aviator (keen, if not always successful – among the items he managed to crash into were the bandstand at Heaton Park, the cucumber frames at Salford racecourse and the River Irwell). The apprentice, a youngster from Old Trafford named John Alcock, nonetheless became infected with the flying bug and, come the First World War, became a bomber pilot. He was later shot down over Turkey and taken prisoner, but returned to England after the conflict.

Arthur Whitten Brown also had Manchester connections, despite being born in Glasgow to American parents. His father was employed by the American company Westinghouse, and was in Scotland to seek out suitable premises for the company. Arthur followed his father into the company, being apprenticed to them at their Manchester works and studying part-time at the city's university. On the outbreak of the First World War he joined the Manchester Regiment, but later transferred to the fledgling Royal Flying Corps where he became a bomber pilot. He too was shot down, badly injured and became a prisoner of war.

Their epic flight took off from St Johns, Newfoundland, on 14 June 1919, in a converted Vickers Vimy bomber.

For over sixteen hours they struggled across the ocean, making an average 115mph headway and contending with hazards such as icing of the engines and fog so dense that, at times, they could not see the plane's propellers. Finally they found themselves over Clifden, Connemara, in Ireland, where they landed on what liked like a flat field. It turned out to be a bog, and the plane ended up on its nose. But both survived, to be presented with the *Daily Mail* prize by Winston Churchill and, a few days later, they were knighted by King George V. Their Manchester connections were also celebrated with a civic reception in the city and, today, a monument to their achievement stands at Manchester airport.

Alcock died in December of that same year, in an air crash while on his way to the Paris Air Show with the new Vickers Viking seaplane. He is buried in Manchester's Southern Cemetery. Brown lived on until 1948 and his final resting place is in Wales.

MANCHESTER'S AIRPORTS

The first airstrip serving Manchester appears to have been at Trafford Park. The first recorded flight to land there (from Liverpool) was on 7 July 1911. It continued until 1917, at which time land near Mauldeth Road was turned into the Alexandra Park Aerodrome, Manchester's first major airfield (what we now know as Hough End playing fields). Within weeks of the First World War ending, on 14 December 1918, a company called the Manchester–London Air Service Limited was being set up to provide a two-hourly service between the two cities, at less than 6*d* a mile. Although the service never materialised, it was a sign of things to come.

Civilian flying was permitted from Alexandra Park from 1 May 1919 when a converted Handley Page 0/400 bomber brought in the first ten fare-paying passengers from London (a 3½ hour flight). Later that month, a scheduled service opened between Manchester, Southport and Blackpool (a 45-minute each way trip for £9.45 return). The pilot on that occasion, Lieutenant-Colonel Sholto Douglas, would later become Chairman of British European Airways. Among the hazards not familiar to modern air travellers were trespassers onto the airfield (including courting couples) and an owner of the land who let out grazing rights on it. Nonetheless, international air travel from Manchester began in October 1922, when Daimler Airway inaugurated a service to Amsterdam (via London) with onward links to Berlin.

Alexandra Park ceased operating in 1924, when the owner of the land (Lord Egerton of Tatton) refused to sell it on a permanent basis for aviation use. It was at this time that Avro acquired farmland at Bramhall that would become Woodford aerodrome. Up to, and during, the Second World War, Avro continued to build their aircraft at their Newton Heath, Chadderton and other factories, before shipping them to Woodford for final assembly, testing and delivery. Meanwhile, the council searched for a suitable replacement for civil flights. It was October 1928 before the choice of Barton, to the west of the city, was made public. The council owned it and believed it could be made into a commercial airfield for an investment of just £100. In the interim a makeshift airfield was created at Wythenshawe, using a barn and a farmhouse as hangar and terminal building.

The council's faith in Barton was to prove unfounded. It opened on 1 January 1930, but business was slow to develop. In 1934 the Dutch airline KLM refused to use it, saying it was too boggy, too small and too prone to bad weather. The council were soon looking for something more suitable. Various options were considered, including a compromise midway between Manchester and Liverpool at Haydock Park racecourse, but in February 1935 the government approved the use of Ringway. The city council agreed (by just one vote) to spend the £179,295 needed to create the airfield (and to commit a further £45,160 expenditure, should air traffic developments warrant it). The first aeroplane landed there in May 1937 and the official opening by Air Minister Sir Kingsley Wood took place in June 1938. Only one overseas service – to Amsterdam – was able to open before the war brought international air travel to an abrupt end. One interesting feature of the early Ringway airport was that the Rylands building in Market Street (currently occupied by Debenhams) had a high-powered beacon on its roof, visible from 60 miles away. This served as a navigational aid to planes coming into Ringway.

During the war years, Ringway was used for a variety of military purposes, including the training of a new force – paratroopers. Over 60,000 paratroopers were trained there and, at its peak, there were 1,500 trainees living there at any one time. It was released for civilian operation early in 1946 and, by June, the first international service – to Paris, in a converted military cargo plane, the Dakota – was inaugurated. Passenger numbers grew rapidly, swamping the pre-war facilities, but post-war austerity made it impossible to make improvements. Even so, 1953 saw the airport become intercontinental, when Belgian airline Sabena opened a service to New York. Passenger numbers were exceeding a million a year by 1962, when the new terminal was finally completed. The airport got its own railway station in 1993 and four years later approval was given for a second runway. By the turn of the century, Manchester airport ranked eighteenth in the world in terms of its passenger volumes. These had risen to over 21 million passengers a year by 2008, passing through three terminals and two runways, and there are plans for this to rise to 50 million by 2030.

THE AVRO MANCHESTER – THE NEARLY AEROPLANE

What was to be one of Manchester's greatest contributions to the Second World War nearly turned out to be a disaster. In 1937, the Ministry had ordered 200 twin-engined bombers from the Avro company off the drawing board. The aircraft – called the Manchester – was the responsibility of Avro's gifted designer Roy Chadwick. It flew well enough, but Chadwick was unhappy with the engines he had been given to work with. The Rolls-Royce Vultures were insufficiently powerful, unreliable and prone to catching fire.

He proposed a new four-engined variant using Rolls-Royce Merlin engines and, without any authority, set his team to work on the redesign. The Ministry was strongly opposed to the idea, since every spare Merlin engine was needed for Spitfires and Hurricanes, but strings were pulled at Rolls-Royce. Engines were obtained for the prototype, which was built in record time, being largely based on the twin-engined model. The Avro Manchester Mark III first flew in January 1941. The plane was an instant success – in addition to being operationally effective, it was also very simple and labour-efficient to build. In the course of the war, 1,080 had been built at Trafford Park alone (7,377 in total). The Avro Shackleton, which developed from it, remained in RAF service until 1990.

One part of the aircraft that did not survive was the name. Perhaps to remove unhappy associations with the two-engined variety (which were withdrawn from service in 1942, after thirty of them had been lost due to engine failure – more than the Germans shot down) the Avro Manchester Mark III became known as the Lancaster.

9

THE THINGS THEY SAY ABOUT MANCHESTER

In this section we look at some of the things that have been said about Manchester (and the Mancunians) over the centuries.

The Anglo-Saxon Chronicle (AD 923)

> In this year after harvest King Edward went with his forces to Thelwall, and commanded the town to be built and occupied and manned, and commanded another force also of Mercians, the while that he sat there to take possession of Manchester, in Northumbria, and repair and man it.

The *Anglo-Saxon Chronicle* was a regularly updated account of events in Anglo-Saxon England, maintained by clerks in various ecclesiastical centres from the 890s onwards. This is a modern translation of the Old English original record.

The Domesday Book (1086)

> The church of St. Mary and the church of St. Michael held in Mamecestre 1 carucate of land free from all customs but the gelt.

A modern translation of the original. A *carucate* is as much land as a man with one plough and eight oxen could plough in a year. For *gelt* read taxes.

From the charter granted by Henry III (1227)

Know ye that we have granted and by this our present charter have confirmed to Robert Greslay that he and his heirs may have forever one fair at his manor of Mamecestre yearly during three days on the eve and on the day and on the morrow of St. Matthew the apostle on condition (that the said fair may not be to the harm of neighbouring fairs).

From the survey of the Manor of Manchester (1322)

There is there the mill of Mamcestre running by the water of Irk worth £10 yearly, to which all the burgesses and all the tenants of the town of Mamcestre with the hamlets of Ardwicke, Oponshaghe, Moston, Nuthurst, Gothereswicke, and Ancottes ought to grind their grain to the sixteenth grain ... There is there the lord's common oven, worth half a mark yearly at which each burgess of Mamcestre ought to bake by custom; and also a certain fulling mill running by the bank of the said water (of Irk) worth 13s 4d yearly; there is also there the mill of Gorton running by the water of Gorrebrocke, worth 40s yearly, at which all the tenants of the said hamlet ought to grind to the sixteenth grain.

Fulling – a process for cleansing and thickening cloth.

Of Oponshaghe. There are there 100 acres of turf moor of the lord's soil which cannot be extended to a yearly profit because its worth decreases yearly so that it will quickly be annihilated; in which the lord's tenants of Gorton, Oponshaghe and Ardwycke and the lords of Ancotes, have common of turbary.

Turbary – the right to dig peat for fuel on common land.

Act of 32 Henry VIII (1540)

The Collegiate Church of Manchester (in common with twenty-seven other places, mainly collegiate) obtained the right of sanctuary constituting it a 'place of privilege ... for term of life, to all offenders and malefactors of whatever quality, kind or nature their offence might be, for which saide offences the pain and punishment of death should ensue by the statute laws and customs of the realm' other than murder, rape, burglary, highway robbery or wilfully burning any house or barn.

This privilege was taken away from the town in the following year.

Leyland Itinerary (c. 1540)

Mamcestre on the south side of the Irwell river, stondeth in Salfordshiret, and is the fairest, best-buildid, quickest and most populous tounne of all Lancastreshire, yet is in hit one Paroch Chirch, but is a College, and almost thorow-howt doble ilyd ex quadrato lapide durissimo, whereof a goodly quarre is hard by the towne. There be divers stone bridges in the towne, but the best of iii arches is over Irwel. This bridge dividith Mancestre from Salford, the wich is a large suburbe to Mancestre. On this bridge is a praty little chapel. (The next is the bridge which is over Hirke river on the which the fair buildid college standeth, as in the very point of the mouth of it. On Hirke river be divers faire mills that serve the town. In the town be two faire market places.) And almost ii flyte shottes without the towne benethe on the same side of Irwel yet be seen the dikes and foundations of Old Man Caltel yn a ground now inclosed. The stones of the ruines of this castel were translated towards making of briddges for the Toune.

The passage in brackets is taken from Aston's *Picture of Manchester* (c. 1817). *Ex quadrato lapide durissimo* translates as very hard stone blocks and *ii flyte shottes* is two bow-shot lengths.

William Camden (1582)

In a park of the Earl of Derby in this neighbourhood called Alparc, I saw foundations of an old square tower, called Mancastle, where the river falls into the Irwell. I do not affirm this to have been the ancient Mancunium, as it encompasses but a small space, but rather some station of the Romans.

William Stukeley Itinerarium Curiosum (1724)

[Manchester is] the largest, most rich, populous and busy village in England having about 2,400 families ... They have looms which work 24 laces at once, which were stolen from the Dutch.

His estimate of the population probably relates to the whole parish. This, and the following two items, illustrates the imprecision of population estimating in these pre-census days.

Daniel Defoe, A Tour Through the Whole Island of Great Britain (1726)

[Manchester is] one of the greatest, if not really the greatest mere village in England. It neither a walled town, city or corporation; they send no members to Parliament; and the highest magistrate they have is a constable or headborough; and yet it has a collegiate church, several parishes, takes up a large space of ground and, including the suburb or the part of the town called Salford over the bridge, it is said to contain above fifty thousand people. I cannot doubt but this increasing town will, some time or other, obtain some better face of government, and be incorporated, as it deserves to be.

Manchester, for the Industry of its Inhabitants, is often compared by Travellers to the most industrious towns of Holland; the smallest children all being employed, and earning their bread.

C. Roeder, visiting the town in 1752

Imagine a sprightly gay, still feudal, little country town, given intensely to trade, its outskirts pretty townships loosely hanging on, divided only by hedges, fields and lanes – the very image of a radiant little garden city. There were only 2,700 to 2,800 houses, two or three storeys high, occupied by some 18,000 souls (Salford, the sister town, included) and sprinkled picturesquely over some 160 small streets, lanes and alleys, broken up pleasantly by interwoven gardens, or large bleaching, dyeing and tenter crofts, where a strong gust sufficed to blow the town clear of the mingling wreath of smoke that curled up from its modest chimneys. Education and leisure for the poor were little known.

Samuel Curwen, Journal and Letters (1777)

The disposition and manners of this people ... are inhospitable and boorish ... In all the manufacturing towns there is a jealousy and suspicion of strangers ... The dress of the people here savours not much of the London mode in general; the people are remarkable for coarseness of feature, and the language is unintelligible ... The ladies, who if they do not a part, are ever violent and scruple not, openly and without restraint, to drink Prince Charlie's health, and express their wishes for his restoration.

Curwen was an American, who happened to visit Manchester just as there was an upsurge of anti-American feeling there, coinciding with the American War of Independence. This may help to account for his jaundiced view of the town.

James Ogden (1783)

The large and populous town of Manchester, has now excited the attention and curiosity of strangers, on account of its extensive trade, and the rapid increase of its buildings, with the enlargement of its streets; being also the first theatre whereon the indefatigable Gilbert and ingenious

Brindley exhibited their amazing talents for the establishment of canals and subterraneous Navigations, under the auspices of that friend to the poor, and patron of mechanic arts, the most noble Duke of Bridgewater ...

P.A. Nemnich (a German visiting Manchester in 1799)

This town is known throughout the world for its cotton manufactures; but it is little more than a name to foreigners. Manchester is very irregularly built, as are almost all towns in England, where the inhabitants site their buildings and houses for the most part according to the convenience of their trade. As can, of course, be expected from such a town, there are many large and beautiful houses. Of the various churches St Peter's is the newest. It is built after the style of the one in Rome, but is very small, and is still without a tower, because, it is said, the subscribers had not enough money. The common people may not frequent this church which is only for gentlemen. The Infirmary is a beautiful, very clean building, equipped according to the most excellent principles; near by are also baths an a lunatic hospital, the best section of which is called the Asylum. There is also a lying-in hospital for poor women. For amusement there are a theatre, concert halls, assembly rooms and so on.

The market place is not sufficiently large or imposing for a town such as Manchester. The centre of it is raised somewhat and is called the Exchange. It is frequented in the middle of the day between 10 and 12.

'In the old College building, which has stood since 1422, is a library which was founded by Humphrey Chetham ... As I went downstairs I saw a swarm of orphans (blue coat boys), with their teacher, on their knees in prayer, in deepest silence. As soon as this mechanical act was over, there was a general cry and the youngsters rushed over tables and benches and pushed out through the door. What I could make out of the words uttered by these many voices was for the most part angry cursing. Then the boys who had been praying went off to play and seemed to find the greatest satisfaction in wrestling. Such lads will make fine fellows later.

The Duke of Bridgewater's Navigation carries goods between Manchester and Liverpool daily except Sundays. In addition three covered boats (passage or pleasure boats) ply to and fro daily in turn to carry passengers and their luggage. At London Bridge Station stage coaches are always ready to carry passengers on to Liverpool.

My plan to make the journey from Manchester to Liverpool by water was frustrated. A heavy downpour of rain, which continued for several days, stopped traffic on the canal which overflowed its banks which were damaged at several places. The damage caused by the flooding was estimated at more than £100,000.

Dr John Aitken (late eighteenth century)

The town has now in every respect assumed the style and manners of one of the commercial capitals of Europe.

This at a time when Manchester was thirty years or more away from being recognised even as a town in local government terms.

The Revd John Clayton (late eighteenth century)

Our streets swarm with distressed objects of every kind; hunger and nakedness, abject misery and loathsome poverty may be found in every neighbourhood.

Clayton was one of those who blamed the poor themselves for their lot, due to their idleness and extravagance and, in particular, their wicked habit of drinking tea.

Thomas de Quincey – romantic writer and opium eater (born 1785)

In this place trade is the Elysium and money is the God. I cannot sit out of doors but I am nosed by a factory, a cotton-boy, a cotton dealer or something else allied to that most detestable commerce.

Joseph Aston, A Picture of Manchester (1819)

Relatively considered, Manchester is situated on low ground: there is a descent to it, which ever way it is approached. The air is, perhaps, too moist, partly owing to its situation, at the junction of three rivers; and partly to its laying so immediately in the vicinity of the range of Yorkshire hills, from which the clouds, gathered over the western ocean, are driven back into the valley; and, perhaps, something ought to be attributed to the circumstance of many of the old streets being built upon morasses, and the site of old pools of water.

The Times on the working people of Manchester (c. 1819)

Their wretchedness seems to madden them against the rich, who they dangerously imagine engross the fruits of their labour without having any sympathy for their wants.

The Times on the New Cross area (1819)

It is occupied chiefly by spinners, weavers ... its present situation is truly heart-rending, overpowering. The streets are confined and dirty; the houses neglected and the windows often without glass. Out of the windows, the miserable rags of the families ... hung up to dry; the household furniture, the bedding, the clothes of the children and the husband were seen at the pawnbrokers.

German visitor, Peter Beuth (1823)

> It is only here, my friend, that the machinery and buildings
> can be found commensurate with the miracles of modern
> times – they are called factories. Such a barn of a place is
> eight or nine storeys high, up to forty windows long and
> usually four windows deep ... in addition, a forest of steam
> engine chimneys, so like needles that one cannot compre-
> hend how they stay up, present a wonderful sight from a
> distance, especially at night when the thousands of win-
> dows are brightly illuminated with gas light.

But the person to whom he sent these thoughts, Karl Schinkel,
came to see them for himself and formed a rather less
favourable view of them, as follows:

Karl Schinkel on Manchester's mills (c. 1823)

> Monstrous shapeless buildings, put up only by foremen
> without architecture, only the least that was necessary and
> out of red brick.

Three views on Manchester and lawlessness

From an 1830 description of Manchester:

> From such a population as that which inhabits Manchester,
> it should scarcely be expected that occasional acts of riot
> and insubordination should not occur.

From *Blackwood* magazine, before 1839:

> All attempts to radicalise Manchester must fail. The working classes are not, on the whole, democratic. Parson Stephens may teach radicalism to a few hundred vagabonds – as Henry Hunt once did the same thing, on the now almost forgotten field of Peterloo. But take the people in a mass in Manchester, they are essentially men of business … this is undoubtedly the cause of their wealth and prosperity – and is one reason why they are pacific and loyal. Occasional ebullitions are but of little real importance. In a few weeks the traitor and the treason are forgotten – and the men return to the power looms, or the self-acting mule.

From Manchester as it is (1839):

> Manchester has, by some means, obtained at a distance, an unenviable notoriety on account of its rioting propensities. It is a matter of observation *at home,* that the exhibition of these propensities is a sure index of *bad times.* When trade is good, and the operative is fully employed, he has neither time nor inclination to grow disorderly; but whenever the reverse is the case – when, for instance the operatives are working 'short time', and they are compelled to live upon half their usual earnings – the circumstances, and the idle time on their hands, are almost sure, among the thousands of men who are here solely dependent upon their daily labour, to produce riotous discontent; and there is never wanting a 'leading spirit' who, more intellectual than the mass, knows how to 'direct the storm', and perhaps scruples not to accelerate the process, in order to derive pecuniary emolument to himself. Such have been the characteristics of several of the Manchester riots.

Manchester as it was (recorded by B. Love in 1839)

> There are many old inhabitants living who recollect the town when very circumscribed in its limits. They remember a time when, for instance, Ardwick Green, now connected to the town by continuous lines of houses, was a long country

walk – when the line of the present substantial warehouses in New Market-Buildings was a pool of water – when the present handsome sheet of water in front of the Infirmary was a stagnant pond – when Oxford-road and Lower Mosley-street, and all the districts beyond, were yet fields and gardens – when High-street and Cannon-street. And the upper end of Market-street, and St Ann's-square, were private dwellings. They can recollect the first factory erected in the town – the one in Miller's-lane – and the crowds of people that flocked to see the high chimney belonging to it, when it was in the progress of erection – they remember Strangeways when a public house, its bowling green and the pile called Strangeways-hall, were the only encroachments on green fields and pastures stretching even to Hunts Bank – they tell of a time when a coach to Liverpool started at six o'clock in the morning, and reached its destination at the same hour in the evening. To the present generation the reminiscences of these not very aged individuals, seem marvellous, but their accuracy is unquestionable.

Archibald Prentice, Manchester 1792–1832 (published 1851)

The volumes of smoke which, in spite of legislation to the contrary, continually issue from factory chimneys, and form a complete cloud over Manchester, certainly make it less desirable as a place of residence than it is as a place of business, and the enjoyment of the inhabitants would be greatly increased, could they breathe a purer atmosphere and have a brighter and more frequent sight of the sun. But, to counterbalance the disadvantage, they have the privilege of walking unrestrainedly through the fine fields of the vicinity; and thousands and tens of thousands whose avocations render fresh air and exercise an absolute necessity of life, avail themselves of the right of footway through the meadows and cornfields and parks in the immediate neighbourhood. There are so many pleasant footpaths, that a pedestrian might walk completely round the town in a circle, which would seldom exceed a radius of 2 miles from the Exchange, and in which he would scarcely ever have occasion to encounter the noise, bustle and dust of a public cart-road or paved street. The beautifully undulating country between the valley of the Irk and Cheetham Hill, the fine valley of the Irwell, with its verdant meadows; the slope from Pendleton to the plain, which commencing between the extremities of Hulme and Chorlton-upon-Medlock, extends south and west over the greater part of Cheshire; all this scenery, which in any country would be admired, but which has a hundred additional charms to him which is condemned, day after day, month after month and year after year to toil in the dirt and smoke of a great town – all this delightful scenery lies open to the pedestrian; and whilst he strays along through the open fields or wooded park, or the narrow and retired lane, and breathes the pure air of heaven, he feels that all these fields, and parks and lanes, are as open to him, and to all those who hang on his arm, or play by his side as if they were his own 'to have and to hold' as long as trees grow or water runs.

Prentice was probably describing Manchester as it was in 1826.

James Kay-Shuttleworth, Four periods of Public Education (c. 1832)

Near the centre of the town, a mass of buildings, inhabited by prostitutes and thieves, is intersected by narrow and loathsome streets, and close courts, defiled with refuse ... In Parliament Street, there is only one privy for 380 inhabitants, which is placed in a narrow passage, whence its effluvia infest the adjacent houses, and must prove a most fertile source of disease ... In Parliament Passage about thirty houses have been erected ... these thirty houses have one privy ...

The state of the streets and the houses in that part of Number 4 district including between Store Street and Travis Street, and London Road is exceedingly wretched ... these avenues are rough, irregular gullies, down which filthy streams percolate; and the inhabitants are crowded in

dilapidated abodes, or obscure and damp cellars, in which it is impossible for the health to be preserved ...

It may suffice to refer generally to the wretched state of the habitations of the poor in Clay Street and the lower portion of Pot Street; in Portugal Street; in Back Hart Street and many of the courts in the neighbourhood of Portland Street, some of which are not more than a yard and a quarter wide, and contain houses, frequently three storeys high, the lowest of which storeys is occasionally used as a recepticle of excrementitious matter.

The following section describes the Little Ireland area, around where Oxford Road station now stands:

The privies are in a most disgraceful state, inaccessible from filth, and too few for the accommodation of the number of people – the average number being 200–250 people. The upper rooms are, with a few exceptions, very dirty and the cellars much worse; all damp and some occasionally overflowed. The cellars consist of two rooms on a floor, each nine to ten feet square, some inhabited by ten persons, other by more: in many, the people have no beds, and keep each other warm by close stowage in shavings, straw, etc.; a change of linen or clothes is an exception to the common practice. Many of the back rooms where they sleep have no other means of ventilation than from the front rooms.

Alexis de Tocqueville (1833–40)

It is in the middle of this vile cesspool that the greatest stream of human industry flows out to fertilise the entire universe. From this filthy sewer flows pure gold. It is here that the human spirit attains almost complete development and at the same time utter brutishness; here, civilisation produces its miracles and civilised man is turned back almost into a savage.

Everything in the exterior appearance of the city attests to the individual powers of man; nothing the directing power of society. At every turn, human liberty shows its capricious creative force. There is no trace of the slow continuous action of Government.

Richard Parkinson, On The Present Condition of the Labouring Poor in Manchester (1841)

[T]here is no town in the world where the barrier between rich and poor is so great, or the barrier between them so difficult to be crossed … The separation between the different classes, and the consequent ignorance of each other's habits and condition, are far more complete in this place than in any country of the older nations of Europe, or the agricultural portions of our own kingdom.

W. Cooke Taylor, Notes on a Tour of the Manufacturing Districts of Lancashire (1842)

I love the men of Manchester but I will not flatter them, and I tell them that they have done much to alienate from them the affection of the working classes. I would say to

them, you have the public places of recreation, Zoological and Botanical Gardens, but have you rendered them
accessible to the operative? Have you not, on the contrary, availed yourself of the most flimsy excuses to shut
every door of recreation against him? Does the working
man believe your excuses? Ask him and he will laugh in
your face.

Leon Faucher, Manchester in 1844

Manchester does not present the bustle either of London
or Liverpool. During the greater part of the day the town
is silent, and appears almost deserted. The heavily laden
boats glide noiselessly along the canals ... The long trains
roll smoothly along the lines of railway ... You hear nothing
but the breathing of the vast machines sending forth fire and
smoke through their tall chimneys.

The town realises in a measure the Utopia of Bentham.
Everything is measured in its results by the standard of utility; and if the BEAUTIFUL, the GREAT and the NOBLE
ever take root in Manchester, they will be developed according to this standard.

Nothing is more curious than the industrial topography of
Lancashire. Manchester, like a diligent spider, is placed at
the centre of the web, and sends forth roads and railways
towards its auxiliaries, formerly villages, but now towns,
which serve as outposts to the grand centre of industry.

[A]t the very moment when the engines are stopped, and
the counting houses closed, everything which was the
thought – the authority – the impulsive force – the moral
order of this immense industrial conurbation, flies from
the town and disappears in an instant. The rich man
spreads his couch amidst the beauties of the surrounding
country, and abandons the town to the operatives, pub-
licans, mendicants, thieves and prostitutes, merely taking
the precaution to leave behind him a police force, whose

duty it is to preserve some little of material order in this pell-mell of society.

Leon Faucher was a French journalist and politician. The reference to Jeremy Bentham relates to his theory of utilitarianism, which held that an action is morally right if it has consequences that lead to happiness and wrong if it brings about the reverse. A society should therefore aim for the greatest happiness for the greatest number. The last quotation refers to the flight of the middle classes from the town. This did indeed provoke a crisis in the governance of the town, with there being not enough people of substance left to fill the elected offices of local government.

J.G. Kohl, Ireland, Scotland and England (1844)

Never since the world began was there a town like it, in its outward appearance, its wonderful activity, its mercantile and manufacturing prosperity, and its remarkable moral and political phenomena.

Dr Carus, a visitor from Saxony (1844)

Manchester is certainly a strange place. Nothing is to be seen but houses blackened by smoke and in the external parts of the towns half empty dirty ditches between smoking factories of different kinds, all built with regard to practical utility and without any respect at al for external beauty ... The light even is quite different from what it is elsewhere. What a curious red colour was presented by the evening light this evening. It is not like a mist nor like a dust nor like smoke but it is a sort of mixture of these three ingredients ...

On approaching the town:

One receives one's first intimation of its existence from the lurid gloom of the atmosphere that hangs over it. There is a murky blot in one section of the sky, however clear the weather, which broadens and heightens as we approach until it seems spread over half the firmament, and now the innumerable chimneys come in view, tall and dim in the dun haze, each bearing atop its own troubled pennant of darkness.

Friedrich Engels, *The Condition of the Working Classes in England in 1844*

Right and left a multitude of covered passages lead from the main streets into the numerous courts, and he who turns in thither gets into a filth and disgusting grime, the equal of which is not to be found. In one of these courts there stands directly at the entrance, at the end of the covered passage, a privy without a door, so dirty that the inhabitants can pass into and out of the court only by passing through foul pools of stagnant urine and excrement. At the bottom flows, or rather stagnates, the Irk, a narrow, coal-black foul-smelling stream, full of debris and refuse, which it deposits on the shallower right bank. Above the bridge are tanneries, bone mills and gas works, from which all drains and refuse find their way into the Irk, which receives further the contents of all the neighbouring sewers and privies.

The New Town is composed of single rows of houses and groups of streets which might be small villages, lying on bare clayey soil which does not produce even a blade of grass. The houses – or rather the cottages – are in a disgraceful state because they are never repaired. They are filthy and beneath them are to be found damp, dirty cellar dwellings; the unpaved alleys lack any form of drainage. The district is infested with small herds of pigs; some of them are penned up in little courts and sties, while others wander freely on the neighbouring hillside. The lanes in this district are so filthy that it is only in very dry weather that one can reach it without sinking ankle-deep at every step. Near St Georges Road these isolated groups of houses are built closer together and one reaches a maze of lanes, blind alleys and back passages and courts. The nearer one gets to the centre of the town, the more closely packed are the houses and the more irregular is the layout of the streets. On the other hand, the streets here are often paved or at least have adequate pavements and gutters; but the filth, and the disgusting conditions of the houses, particularly the cellars, remain unchanged.

Chorlton-on-Medlock, Ardwick, Cheetham Hill and Pendleton, where the merchants lived, had:

free, wholesome country air, fine comfortable houses ... and the finest part of the arrangement is this, that the members of the monied aristocracy can take the shortest road through the middle of all the labouring districts to their places of business without ever seeing that they are in the midst of the grimy misery that lurks to the right and to the left.

Owing to the curious layout of the town it is quite possible for someone to live for years in Manchester and to travel daily to or from his work without ever seeing a working class quarter or coming into contact with an artisan. He who visits Manchester simply on business or for pleasure need never see the slums, mainly because the working-class districts and the middle-class districts are quite distinct. This distinction is due partly to deliberate policy and partly to instinctive and tacit agreement between the two social groups. In those area where the two social groups happen to come into contact with each other the middle-classes sanctimoniously ignore the existence of their less fortunate neighbours.

... the main streets which run from the Exchange in all directions out of the town are occupied almost uninterruptedly on both sides by shops, which are kept by members of the lower middle classes. In their own interests these shopkeepers should keep the outsides of their shops in a clean and respectable condition, and in fact they do so. Those shops which are situated in the vicinity of commercial or middle-class residential districts are more elegant than those which serve as a façade for the workers' grimy cottages. Nevertheless even the less pretentious shops adequately serve their purpose of hiding from the eyes of wealthy ladies and gentlemen with strong stomachs and weak nerves the misery and squalor which are part and parcel of their own riches and luxury.

The first English edition of Engels' book was not published until 1892. In the preface to it he wrote:

The most crying abuses described in this book have either disappeared or have been made less conspicuous. But what of that? Whole districts which in 1844 I could describe as almost idyllic have now with the growth of the towns fallen into the same state of dilapidation, discomfort and misery.

Benjamin Disraeli, Coningsby (1844):
In Disraeli's novel, the character Coningsby says, 'What would I not give to see Athens?' 'I have seen it,' was the reply, 'The age of ruins is past. Have you seen Manchester? Manchester is as great a human exploit as Athens.'

E.D. Simon and J. Inman, The Rebuilding of Manchester (1935)

Manchester shared to the full in the new movement towards housing reform; there must have been some very progressive members on the City Council at the time. In 1867 they obtained a local Act of Parliament which was the first to lay down that houses which are 'unfit for habitation' shall be closed without compensation to their owners. The Town Clerk of Smethwick writes 'It is surely a monumental tribute to the prescience of the public administration in Manchester as far back as 1867 that, by the epoch-making Manchester Improvement Act of that year, there was planted the root-stock from which has sprung the whole slum-clearance legislation of this country'.

A.J.P. Taylor, Encounter magazine (March 1957)

Manchester is as distinctive in its ways as Athens or Peking. It is the symbol of a civilisation which was, until recently, an ambition of mankind, though now little more than a historical curiosity.

Manchester is the only English city that can look London in the face, not merely as a regional capital, but as a rival version of how men should live in a community.

Manchester is irredeemably ugly. There is no spot to which you could lead a blindfolded stranger and say happily: 'Now open your eyes'. Norman Douglas had a theory that English people walked with their eyes on the ground so as to avoid the excrement of dogs on the pavement. The explanation in Manchester is simpler: they avert their eyes from the ugliness of their surroundings.

The people, too, are remarkably unattractive in appearance. When I was a lecturer at Manchester, I used to peer along the serried rows of note-takers in the hope of finding a pretty girl. The only one I ever spotted turned out to be an Italian visitor. No doubt Puritanism makes the women dress so badly. The stunted growth of men and women alike is said to be due either to their Danish ancestors who settled in the Mersey valley or to the long hours spent by more recent forebears in the cotton factories.

Asa Briggs, Victorian Cities (1968)

With no adequate police, no effective machinery of local government, a disturbed social system which lacked the 'benevolent influence' of 'natural gradations', and an economy subject to fluctuations and developing on the basis of obvious conflicts of interests, Manchester was felt to provide a persistent threat to that 'good order' on which statesmen and moralists loved to dwell.

10

DIRTY OLD TOWN

Severe pollution was one of the prices that Manchester paid
for the more or less unregulated early growth of the Industrial
Revolution. Here we look at the consequences of air and
water pollution and at the corporation's sometimes less than
inspired efforts to deal with these, along with the quantities of
waste produced by an ever-growing population.

WATER

Manchester had its own public water supply from as early as
1506. It came from a spring or fountain in the town centre
(from where we get the name of Fountain Street) and ran,
partly in wooden pipes and partly in an open conduit, to
Market Place, near the cathedral. The supply was limited – in
1578 the authorities restricted each household to 'No more
than could be contained in a vessel that one woman was able
to carry on her head', and access to it was limited to certain
times of day. Nor can the quality of the water have been very
high; in 1626 they found it necessary to ban 'the washing or
cleansing of calves' heads, meat, linen or woollen clothes in
the open part of the conduit on penalty of a fine of twelve
pence'. In 1776 the conduit collapsed and even this inadequate
supply was denied the town.

The alternatives were not attractive; wells sunk into the red
sandstone on which the town was built yielded a water supply

that was hard, impure and injurious to health (some of the wells were polluted by contact with graveyards, and generally the water was said to make Mancunians particularly liable to 'glandular obstructions and scrophulous swellings'). Nor was the collection of rainwater to be recommended; as early as the seventeenth century it was described as falling 'as black as ink' and it needed to be allowed to settle before any use could be made of it. Water carriers and water carts plied the streets with an alternative supply, and some poor souls even relied on the filthy contents of the River Medlock or the canals. Small wonder that the theft of water became the town's most common form of larceny.

At about the time of the conduit's collapse, the Lord of the Manor installed a pumping engine by the River Medlock, which delivered a water supply to reservoirs at Holt Town near Beswick, from where it was piped around town. But the town was about to be subjected to a huge fraud. In 1808 the Stone Pipe Company was allowed to set up the Manchester

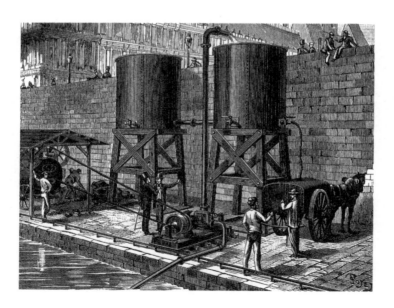

and Salford Waterworks Company. The chief object of the parent company was to sell the town over-priced and defective water pipes cut from solid stone. A 60-mile network of these was supplied and laid. Few were even connected with the water supply, and many of those that were proved incapable of withstanding the water pressure. They compounded the fraud by selling the Waterworks Company their rights to 'The ancient waterworks at Manchester' (which the town might have thought they already owned). The entire network had to be relaid with (cheaper and more reliable) cast iron pipes.

As the town grew, the authorities were forced to look further afield for an unpolluted water supply and, by 1823, larger reservoirs were being built at Gorton. Even so, by 1840 the waterworks company still served less than a quarter of the town's houses and there was just one water closet for every ten households. The corporation decided in 1846 to end years of unsatisfactory service by the Waterworks Company by taking it into public ownership. Water engineer John Bateman was brought in to advise on how to improve supplies and he recommended bringing it in from the Longdendale Valley in Derbyshire. This was done and supplies started flowing by 1851. But, within just a few years, even the 8,000,000 gallons a day this could provide was starting to look inadequate. After much corporation dithering, a plan was drawn up to take water from Thirlmere in the Lake District. The scheme got through parliament in 1879, but it took until 1894 for the first 96-mile pipeline to be completed.

RIVERS

For a long time there was no effective control over the use of Manchester's rivers. Businesses and private individuals could extract from them, discharge waste into them or dam them up as they saw fit. The result was that they became horrific open sewers, as vividly described in this Parliamentary Commissioner's report of 1851:

In Manchester, the water thus tainted (by sewage and industry) is further used for condensing and other purposes in steam engines and is discharged heated, back into the open or covered water courses, which also receive the drainage of this large town, so that a semi-liquid compound is formed, an accurate idea of which no written description can convey. A thick scum coats the surface, upon and over which birds can walk; the putrid carcasses of dead animals, dogs, cats, etc. float and rot in the midst; fermentation takes place rapidly, as large bubbles of gas may be seen escaping, and a thick vapour hangs over the entire area.

One particularly gruesome event followed floods in July 1872, when the waters lifted fifty coffins from the cemetery and swept them down the River Medlock. It was recognised as early as the mid-nineteenth century that the solution to the main problem would be a proper system of intercepting sewers, but the corporation shied away from the cost of this (estimated at £100,000 – albeit a fraction of the cost to the community of the water-based epidemics that regularly hit the town). In fact, the corporation went the other way and sought to impose a tax on anyone installing a water closet in their house. The 'logic' for this was, first, that each new WC put an additional strain on the town's already over-stretched water supplies and, secondly, that until a comprehensive system was in place, new WCs would further add to the discharges into the waterways. Under the old arrangements, most households had their sewage collected (albeit infrequently and inadequately) by the night-soil men, who carted it away in stinking vehicles known as Dolly Vardens (an ironic reference to a popular perfume of the day).

Small wonder that Manchester in the 1860s had the highest death-rate in the country. The council was repeatedly challenged over its inactivity and employed every spurious argument it could for inaction, even down to blaming the town's problems on the filthy and depraved habits of its residents (who, they said, could not be trusted with a technological advance like a water closet). When the Suez Canal was opened in 1869, satirical locals christened the River Irwell the Sewage Canal. Attempts were made in 1878 to set up a joint sewerage scheme with neighbouring authorities, but this time it was the neighbours' turn to baulk at the cost, and the scheme was only partially carried out by 1894.

In the end, it took a mixture of shaming and blackmail to stir the council into action. The Ship Canal Company was never best pleased with the way the city polluted its waterway (the official opening of the Ship Canal by Queen Victoria was nearly postponed for this reason) and the Mersey and Irwell Joint Board eventually prosecuted the council for pollution. The magistrates fined them and, more importantly, made it clear that if nothing were done, further and increasing fines would be imposed on a daily basis. Faced with the prospect of potentially limitless fines, the council had little choice but to find the money to complete the scheme. In 1904, the city finally got the sewerage system people began campaigning for a lifetime earlier.

AIR POLLUTION

Manchester sits in a hollow, where it retains most of its own smoke and collects some of its neighbours' on the prevailing winds. The authorities identified air pollution as a problem as long ago as 1800:

> The increase of steam engines as well as smoak issuing from chimneys used over stoves, foundries, dressers, dyehouses and bakehouses are become a great nuisance to the town unless so constructed as to burn the smoak arising from them which might be done at moderate expense.

J.G. Kohl reported in 1844 that:

> The blue heavens above are hidden from us by the thick smoke of the huge factory chimneys which weave a close impenetrable veil of brown fog between the city and the sky.

In 1848, a strange indication of the growing problem came with the discovery in Manchester of the dark carbonara form of the peppered moth. This normally light-coloured creature had responded to its murky surroundings by developing a darker variety to give it more effective camouflage. It was around this time too that a scientist working in Manchester, Robert Smith, first identified the phenomenon of acid rain.

Early attempts to legislate against the smoke nuisance proved ineffective, and it took until 1874 for the council to appoint just two factory chimney inspectors to cover the entire city. Not surprisingly, the Noxious Vapours Abatement Association criticised them in 1891 for only prosecuting a tiny proportion of offenders (though the council also had the Chamber of Commerce warning them that over-zealous enforcement would drive business out of the city). When the Smoke Abatement League of Great Britain was formed in 1909, it was only fitting that it should base its headquarters in Manchester. Even so, action was still decades away and Manchester was just about to introduce the world's first smokeless zone when the Second World War intervened.

The council finally got local powers to introduce smokeless zones in 1946, and 104 acres of the city centre were designated in 1952. But it took the 4,000 deaths in the London smog that same year to bring about national legislation – the 1956 Clean Air Act. At last Manchester could take concerted action with its neighbours against a nuisance which, more than almost any other, did not recognise local authority boundaries. Virtually all of Manchester was a smokeless zone by 1981.

But this was not to say that Manchester had solved its air pollution problem. Clean air legislation and the switch to different kinds of heating fuel has largely dealt with the problem of sulphurous smog, but the enormous growth in car ownership led to a corresponding increase in photochemical smog. Once again, a Europe-wide study found that Manchester had the dubious distinction of being the worst sufferer from the problem.

RUBBISH

Manchester had its own dustmen as early as the eighteenth century. A local Act of 1792 established a weekly collection of people's refuse. However, having collected it, the dustmen used to dump it somewhat haphazardly – in some cases, like in Holt Town, in the middle of busy residential neighbourhoods, to the fury of the locals. It was in Holt Town too, that the city's first refuse disposal works – an early incinerator – was opened in 1878. Thousands of tons of refuse was also dumped on large bog-land estates owned by the council, like Chat Moss and Carrington Moss, incidentally turning them into fertile and profitable farmland.

Street cleaning was more of an essential in the days when most of the traffic was horse-drawn, but it tended to be the most affluent streets (which arguably needed it least) that got the most frequent attention. Some of the worst areas, the courts in the slums for instance, were classed as private spaces and therefore got no publicly-funded cleaning at all. In the 1830s, the authorities used to employ some of the able-bodied inmates of the workhouse as street cleaners (or 'scavengers') for a wage of 1s a week (with tools and topcoat provided).

11

CHARITABLE MANCHESTER

In the days before the public purse provided much of the care for people's needs, charitable works and public subscriptions raised the money to fund a remarkable variety of worthy causes in the town. Some of these are discussed below.

HUGH OLDHAM AND MANCHESTER GRAMMAR SCHOOL

Hugh Oldham, the Bishop of Exeter and a man who came from Manchester, founded the nation's first free grammar school in the town. He was concerned that Lancashire boys, 'Having pregnant wits have been for the most part brought up rudely and idley and not in virtue, cunning, erudition, literature and good manners', and the 1525 charter for the school (written just after Oldham's death) aimed to ensure that the pupils grew up to 'Know, love, honour and dread God and his laws.' The school's income came from property rentals and the income from three mills serving the town, and they adopted the Bishop's badge and his motto *Sapere aude* – 'dare to be wise'. Oldham, though no intellectual himself (he was described as having 'more zeal than knowledge, more devotion than learning') was nonetheless an enthusiastic promoter of education. He also played an important part in the foundation of not one but two Oxford colleges, Corpus Christi and Brasenose.

The school was based in Long Millgate and was open and free of charge to any boy with the right academic background. Poor pupils could help cover their living expenses by cleaning the school. Two restrictions to admission applied; no child carrying a weapon would be admitted (something that was breached when the pupils staged a sit-in involving the use of firearms in 1690 – students knew how to organise a protest in those days), nor would anyone be admitted suffering from any 'Horrible or contagious infirmity infective, such as pox, leprosy, pestilence for the time being'.

Pupils got just four days leave at Christmas and Easter, plus holy days; school hours ran from 7 a.m. (or 6 a.m. in summer) to 5 p.m. Latin was spoken at all times on school premises and a good deal of the curriculum seemed to involve religious ceremony, including praying for the souls of Hugh Oldham and other departed benefactors of the school. The school was rebuilt in situ in 1776 but shortly afterwards began considering a move, as the encroaching industrialisation made conditions in Long Millgate intolerable – filthy, impoverished and heavily polluted. However, it took them 120 years – until 1931 – to complete their move to their present site in Fallowfield.

HUMPHREY CHETHAM

One pupil of the grammar school, who went on to become a wealthy businessman, was Humphrey Chetham. In 1654, he funded what was probably the world's first free public library next to the school and a bluecoat orphanage for forty poor boys – or, as he put it 'Children of honest, industrious and pains-taking parents and not of wandering, or idle beggars, or rogues.' By the eighteenth century the school roll was between 50 and 100 pupils at any given time, about four of whom would win exhibitions to Oxford or Cambridge each year.

In addition to his business interests (which earned him enough to buy – with his brother – Clayton Hall and its estates) Chetham was appointed High Sheriff of Lancashire in 1634. It was a post forced upon him, for its duties included the collection of the hated Ship Money (a tax used, among other things, by Charles I to collect revenue without having to secure parliamentary approval). More recently, the school has, since 1969, operated as a co-educational music school.

ROYAL INFIRMARY AND OTHER MEDICAL SERVICES

Many attempts had been made to establish a hospital in the town before 1752, when a local businessman, Joseph Bancroft, agreed to fund the expenses of an infirmary for a year. His condition was that Dr Charles White would work for it. White was, for more than sixty years, the town's first surgeon, and a specialist in obstetrics with an international reputation (his father, Thomas, had also been renowned as

a 'male midwife'). He helped bring about a major decrease
in infant mortality. Curiously, Bancroft was to hold the title
of honorary surgeon at the hospital until 1790 (at least, one
hopes the position was genuinely honorary!).

A building was found at Garden Street, Shudehill – albeit with
a capacity of just 12 patients – and they opened for business
in June 1752. In the first year, 75 in-patients and 249 out-
patients were treated (nobody could be admitted, except
on the recommendation of a trustee or other benefactor of
the hospital). Demand quickly outstripped the capacity of
these premises and, in 1754, land at what is now Piccadilly
Gardens (a former claypit, known as the Daube Holes, then
on the outskirts of the town) was acquired from the Lord of
the Manor, Sir Oswald Mosley. The building they planned
to put on it would take 40 in-patients (a number rapidly
revised up to 80). Despite only having £250 towards its cost
when the foundation stone was laid, the building was opened
by 1755. It originally had six physicians and six surgeons,
apparently selected by ballot, along with visiting apothecaries.

Treatment was restricted not least by the infirmary's limited finances. They administered some 40 to 50 gallons of cod liver oil per year as a treatment for rheumatism. The great advantage of this remedy is that it is cheap; its main drawback is that it is totally ineffective as a cure for rheumatism. However, they were luckier than it might seem, since cod liver oil is good for rickets (a disease then often mistaken for rheumatism).

The present Royal Infirmary building along the Oxford Road was opened by King Edward VII in July 1909, offering double the capacity of the old buildings and providing new facilities, like X-rays. The twelve beds provided in the original infirmary have now grown to over 750.

Other medical facilities followed. A lunatic asylum – said to offer a better standard of care than most private establishments – was established in 1766. It operated a humane regime, ruling that:

> No stripes or beatings and no painful coercion whatsoever more than what is necessary to restrain the furious from hurting themselves or others shall be inflicted or made use of by the keeper or any of the servants unless by special order in writing by the physician.

This did not prevent the local press in 1774 from running 'false and scandalous stories' about barbarities in the asylum – claiming that one patient had had his arm broken, another stabbed by a fellow inmate and a third driven to suicide. The asylum moved to Cheadle in Cheshire in 1849.

A dental hospital was opened in 1883. It was around this time that the first Register for Licensed Dentists was created, in an attempt to drive out the many unqualified quacks who posed as dentists. The dental hospital became an important centre for training. One important development was the decision to open evening dental clinics for the many working people who could not afford the time off work (and loss of pay) involved in getting treatment during the working day. By 1887, most of the more than 10,000 patients they treated each year attended the evening surgeries.

When the Royal Manchester Children's Hospital opened in 1829, it was the only establishment in the country specialising solely in the treatment of children. Booth Hall Children's Hospital in Blackley was a product of the generosity of Humphrey Booth, who provided the land and some of the buildings that began treating children in 1908 (switching their attention to wounded soldiers in the First World War).

THE HOUSE OF RECOVERY

This was at Aytoun Street/Portland Street and was established in 1796. Many of its inmates were taken from 'crowded and confused neighbourhoods', where the potential for transmitting disease was great and the prospects of recovering from it correspondingly small. Less than 10 per cent of those admitted to the House of Recovery died of their illness. In the first twenty years of its operation, it nursed over 6,500 patients to recovery and probably saved ten times that number from contracting disease. Despite the good work that institutions like these did, during the 1832 cholera epidemic wild rumours spread through the town that patients were being murdered by the staff. A mob attacked one of the premises and threatened to lynch the staff. Only the intervention of the military restored order.

THE LOCK HOSPITAL

The Lock Hospital in Lloyd Street:

> Affords relief and shelter to females who have been induced to quit their homes and near connexions, by the seductive wiles of men as destitute of feeling and principle, as they were that thought and discretion which might have preserved them from contamination and final loss of character.

> Women without shelter, diseased and in a state of entire destitution, against whom every door was closed, have presented themselves at the New Bailey, and implored to be received as prisoners.

In modern parlance, it was a hospital for venereal diseases. The infirmary would not treat these cases as in-patients, not least because of fears that it might cause a loss of 'respectable' subscriptions to their mainstream medical services. (They did, however, make the concession in 1758 that any sufferers from venereal disease who 'have contracted the distemper innocently' could enter the infirmary, though how doctors were to establish their state of innocence or otherwise is not clear.) Many victims of these diseases were forced to resort to self-diagnosis and medication, or to visiting the various quack 'doctors' who peddled cure-alls for them. Others were driven into the arms of the workhouse.

It was founded in 1819 and went through a long series of financial crises throughout the nineteenth century as it struggled to compete with what many donors might have regarded as more 'worthy' causes. This was despite the fact that a subscription to the hospital entitled the donor to nominate one or more patients for treatment. An earlier establishment, founded in 1774, was forced to close after three years for lack of funds. But this one survived to become St Luke's Hospital and, eventually, part of the National Health Service.

ASYLUM FOR FEMALE PENITENTS

Also known rather forbiddingly as the Penitentiary, this institution was founded in 1822 and was located first in Chorlton-on-Medlock and then in Embden Place, Greenheys. At the end of 1838, it had 47 resident penitents and, apparently, room for a good many more. It was the main charity in Manchester for the rescue of prostitutes and was closely associated with the Lock Hospital. The regime in these establishments was very strict and the house rules typically included:

No conversations with anyone except in the presence of the matron.

No leaving the premises unless accompanied by the matron or her nominee.

No mail to come in or go out except via the matron.

Any deliveries to the inmates to be inspected by matron.

Any games or books to be approved by matron.

No strong liquor.

Two church services daily.

Work to be undertaken and strict hours of getting up and retiring observed.

THE EYE INSTITUTION

Founded in 1814 when W.J. Wilson, a well-known local oculist, proposed setting up a charity to provide eye treatment for those who could not afford to pay for it themselves. It started life in King Street, then moved to several other sites before locating in 1886 at the junction of Nelson Street and Oxford Road. The £25,000 cost of the new building was funded by the local authorities, trade unions and private benefactors.

THE NIGHT ASYLUM

This was opened in February 1838 to serve the destitute poor in Smithfield. Its aim was 'to provide an asylum, during the rain and chilling blasts of a winter's night, to the aged, the destitute, and the stranger in distress'. In its first twelve months its services were called upon by some 17,000 people, including 2,523 children.

THE MANCHESTER AND SALFORD TOWN MISSION

Based in Charlotte Street and founded in 1837, its purpose was 'to bring sinners to the Saviour, and to lead them to take His word as a light to their feet and a lamp to their path'. Each of their missionaries would be attached to groups of about 500 households and would go from house to house, reading scriptures and discussing religious subjects, holding prayer meetings, promoting Sunday Schools, distributing religious tracts and visiting the sick.

MANCHESTER AND SALFORD TEMPERANCE SOCIETY

The temperance movement in Britain had taken its lead from a similar body, established in Boston, USA, in 1826. Manchester's first public meeting to promote the cause was held in May 1830, and their original pledge was to 'abstinence from ardent spirits and moderation in fermented beverages'. By 1835, any suggestion of moderation was abandoned in favour of 'abstinence from all intoxicating liquors'. Fifteen branches of the movement were swiftly formed in Manchester and, by 1839, nationwide membership figures had reached around 500,000. Their weekly journal, the *Star*, by this time boasted a circulation of some 300,000.

DISTRICT PROVIDENT SOCIETY

The society was based in St James' Square, and its aim was:

> To elevate and improve the condition of the working classes, and to assist in conveying the offerings of private benevolence into a proper and deserving channel. Through the medium of domiciliary visiting, the Society seeks to cultivate a kindly feeling between the rich and the poor;

and to improve the condition of the latter by encouraging cleanly, provident and contented habits.

It also had as its aim to discourage the practice of indiscriminate alms-giving.

THE STRANGERS' FRIEND SOCIETY

This society was founded in Manchester by the Methodists in 1791. Its aim was to 'Seek out Misery and give Relief, the succour the stranger, sunk in friendless Poverty and to afford that immediate assistance which urgent want demands.' In practical terms, it meant providing food, bedding, clothing, coals and access to the medical facilities of the infirmary.

EDUCATIONAL BODIES

Long before it became a national requirement to provide primary education for all, Manchester had a variety of initiatives in operation. In 1839, there were a number of infant schools in place, with a total of about 2,000 pupils attending them. One of them, at Saville Street, off Oxford Road in Chorlton-in-Medlock, had been founded in 1823. It was regarded as a particularly good model and was widely visited by educationalists and other interested parties from outside the town. In November 1837, a Manchester Society for Promoting National Education was established, with the aim of making it a national requirement to provide a system of education 'to fit people for the right discharge of the various duties of their station.'

The Factory Act of 1833 was the first to secure any kind of effective trade-off between the employment of young people and their education. It secured the exclusion of children under nine from factories and limited the working hours of children under thirteen to forty-eight hours a week, or nine a day. Children under thirteen were also required to attend school for not less than two hours a day. Importantly, it also introduced inspectors to ensure compliance with the regulations. The reality was that there was no supply of teachers, no funding and precious little enforcement and the 'education' (if it happened at all) could amount to little more than child-minding by an illiterate adult. On the bright side, Manchester's inspector, Leonard Horner, Esq., was at least able to point to twenty-nine establishments where the educational provisions of the Act 'Have been observed in the most efficient manner'. Just over 1,800 children were being educated in these establishments. The curriculum varied widely, from just reading, to include reading, writing, arithmetic, geography, sewing, knitting and (in one case) singing. Most of the schools were within the mills themselves and in just over half of the twenty-nine, the whole cost of them was met by the employer. In others, the pupils were contributing up to 4*d* a week towards the cost.

SUNDAY SCHOOLS AND OTHER PLACES OF LEARNING

Before compulsory primary schooling came in in 1870, most Manchester children's best chance of acquiring any education at all were the church Sunday schools. A survey by the Manchester Statistical Society in 1834 found that some 33,196 children were attending the town's eighty-six Sunday schools, where they would have learned the rudiments of writing and sufficient reading skills to be able to study the scriptures. As a basis for comparison, only 18,661 of Manchester's children were at that time attending a day school of any description, and many of these would have been at what were often hopelessly inadequate Dame Schools. It was said of the women or old men who taught at many of these establishments that their 'Only qualification for this employment seems to be their unfitness for every other.'

RAGGED SCHOOLS

These were another way of providing a basic education to poor children in the days before universal state education (and, indeed, after it – the last one in Manchester was opened as late as 1936). A group of evangelical Christians opened the Sharp Street Ragged School in 1854, the first of thirty-nine to be established in Manchester. They saw it as a form of missionary work to give the children a basic training in reading, writing and arithmetic, along with religious and moral education. Charter Street Ragged School (founded 1861) had rather wider ambitions, providing food, clothing and footwear for the children, and teaching skills such as carpentry and cooking that would be directly useful to them in the labour market.

THE DEAF AND DUMB SCHOOL

It was founded in 1823 and, from 1878, occupied premises at Grosvenor Street, All Saints, near the Oxford Road. At the time of the 1871 census, the school had a total of 138 pupils.

ADULT EDUCATION

The Atheneum gave its middle-class subscribers paying 30s a year access to a library of almost 4,000 volumes, a reading room that subscribed to forty-three English newspapers, lessons in French and Italian and occasional concerts, all housed in a building on Princess Street (dating from 1839) designed by Sir Charles Barry. (Barry got the commission to design the new Houses of Parliament in London just as work commenced on the Atheneum.) Many of the town's great and good were associated with the Atheneum, including Richard Cobden and Robert Owen, and Charles Dickens and Benjamin Disraeli were guests at their first annual soiree in 1843.

For those of a more proletarian inclination (or a more limited budget) 5s a quarter bought them membership of the **Mechanics' Institute** ('For the diffusion of useful knowledge and the encouragement of the educable working class'). The purpose of this was 'to instruct the working classes in the principles of the arts they practice, and in other branches of useful knowledge, excluding party politics and controversial theology'. From it 'a workman may not only acquire a more thorough knowledge of his business, and also a greater degree of skill in the practice of it, but will also be better qualified to advance himself in the world; better qualified to secure the means of support and enjoyment, and better qualified to promote the education of his children.'

In fact, the institute (the first of its kind outside London) offered a wide range of evening courses in the three R's, languages, drawing, gymnasia and vocal music. From 1834, they also founded a day school for 210 boys, and later 100 girls. The organisation started life in 1825 on Cooper Street, before relocating to a new, larger building on Princess Street in 1854.

Somewhat similar in purpose was the **Ancoats Lyceum**, based at 107 Great Ancoats Street. There, for 2s a quarter (1s 6d for females) there was access to a library and news room, a coffee room, and 'weekly meetings for friendly intercourse and mutual improvement, classes for children and adults and lectures on subjects of popular interest.' This body appeared to have a particular interest in its female clientele, since it advertised that its classes were 'attended by a competent female teacher and periodically visited by a committee of ladies'.

Those of an artistic persuasion might have looked towards the **Royal Manchester Institution**. It started out purely as the Manchester Institution in 1823, 'To encourage literature, science and the arts'. A particular feature of the institution was regular art exhibitions, including loans from the private collections of the great and the good, including the Duke of Wellington and Lord Francis Egerton. Their headquarters from 1829 was the Charles Barry-designed building in Mosley Street that now houses the City Art Gallery. The RMI transferred to the corporation in 1882, on condition that it spent £4,000 a year for the next twenty years to add to the art collection.

Scientists would have gravitated towards the **Literary and Philosophical Society**. Established in 1781, they published a number of important scientific papers over the years, including Dalton's discovery of Atomic Theory.

Whitworth Art Gallery and Park. When industrialist Sir Joseph Whitworth died, he established a trust, with the purpose of displaying fine art and providing facilities for the study of the arts. It became part of the University of Manchester in 1958. Whitworth Park was acquired by the corporation from the Whitworth trustees in 1904, to provide some open space in this densely built-up area.

Francis Crossley, founder of the gas engine company that bore his name, was an evangelical Christian and an admirer of William Booth and the Salvation Army. From 1889, he developed a range of social amenities in the Pollard Street area of Ancoats, including meeting rooms, bathing facilities and a coffee tavern. He quit his home in suburban Bowden to live in Star Hall in Pollard Street and, on his death, left it to the Salvation Army as a base for their missionary work.

Ancoats had another benefactor in **Thomas Coglan**. He re-used Ancoats Hall, the former home of mill owner George Murray, as an art gallery. From 1886 to 1954 this was open to all at no charge. The Ancoats Brotherhood also provided an ambitious range of lectures, debates and excursions for working people, that managed to attract some of the leading lights of the day – George Bernard Shaw, William Morris and G.K. Chesterton, among others – to their meetings.

ENVIRONMENTAL IMPROVEMENTS

Public subscription, rather than individual acts of generosity, was the means by which some of the environmental improvements to the town were achieved. For example, in March 1755 the public were invited to subscribe to the widening and improvement of some of the main streets in the town centre – including Old Millgate, St Mary's Gate and the area between the Exchange and St Ann's Square. 80 per cent of the money required was raised within fourteen days, well before the Act of Parliament needed to empower the town's authorities to carry out the works had been obtained.

MANCHESTER'S HOME-MADE ARMY

Public subscription was also used to kit out an army of Manchester volunteers in 1804, when Napoleon was threatening invasion. £22,000 was raised from patriotic citizens, to equip those of the 5,816-man force who could not afford their own uniforms and weapons. In addition, Pickfords, the locally-based hauliers, promised to place 400 horses, 50 wagons and 28 boats at the government's disposal, should the invasion threat materialise. These volunteer militias were not always an unmixed blessing. As the tragic events of the Peterloo Massacre were to show, they could be ill-disciplined, politically motivated and liable to panic.

12

GRAND DESIGNS

> Today our country is at the beginning of the great transi-
> tion from war to peace, and all thinking people will wish
> to inquire about the sort of world to be built for posterity
> ... The extent to which the Civic Authorities will be able to
> re-model Manchester as a fairer city with greatly improved
> living and working conditions will depend ultimately on the
> interest, determination and wishes of the citizens ...
> Mayor's preface to the 1945 *City of Manchester Plan*

As the tide of the Second World War changed, people could
start to look forward to the return to peace. Even before the
war, Manchester had faced some huge challenges, with its vast
areas of outworn slum housing and declining industry. The
wartime years of no investment and the destruction wrought
by the Luftwaffe had only made the problems greater and
more urgent.

As early as August 1941, Lord Reith had advised local
authorities to develop a plan for post-war reconstruction,
and the city council was able to publish this to coincide with
the end of hostilities in 1945. It truly was a grand design,
involving, among other things, moving 120,000 of its
citizens to new or expanded towns some distance from the
city. It had the confidence to forecast what the world would
be like up to fifty years into the future. Unsurprisingly, many
of those forecasts were to prove wildly inaccurate. Given its
radical nature, what is particularly surprising is that they

were allowed to publish it before it had even been considered by any council committee.

It seemed that no assumption was too sweeping, and no detail too minute to escape the plan's attention. Parts of it looked forward fifty years into the 1990s and predicted not just the size, but the age and sex structure of the city's population, how many cars they would own and even how far apart they would drive those cars. On car ownership, they thought that it would peak by about 1970, with there being about one car for every 7.5 people, far lower than official government forecasts. This would give traffic at about twice the pre-war level – another vast under-estimate. But would the city's roads have room for even these lower volumes of traffic? They reminded the readers that, even before the war, the city had felt it was on the brink of gridlock, and only wartime restrictions on motoring had prevented it happening. But at least they rightly identified that a large part of the problem was less to do with the capacity of the roads and more about how they were used. The absence of bypasses meant that large volumes of through traffic, with no reason to visit the city centre, were being drawn through it. Also, the more or less total absence of kerbside parking restrictions meant that much of the capacity of the main roads was taken up by stationary vehicles. They also proposed novel means of hastening the flow of traffic through the city, such as roundabouts – 'Roundabouts of adequate dimensions are still rare in this country, although they were coming into more general use just before the war.'

Another form of traffic whose growth they got wrong was of the winged variety:

> We may therefore have to reckon a few years hence with an extensive use of air liners, with air taxis stationed on flat-roofed buildings, and with folding-winged aeroplanes housed in private garages ... Although Manchester is unlikely to be used as a terminal for transatlantic journeys, it is probable that air services to all Major European cities will become an established part of the city's commercial life.

They forecast some 45,000 passengers a year going through Ringway by 1951. As we saw earlier, the latest forecast of Ringway's traffic is 50 million by 2030.

Some of the possibilities they contemplated seem to us today like simple vandalism. One option they floated was the demolition of the city's most iconic Victorian building, the Town Hall, and its replacement with some hideous municipal swimming bath style of civic building, standing at the head of a boulevard straight out of a Communist dictator's design guide. More generally, they are dismissive of the city's built heritage – 'The city's buildings, with few exceptions, are undistinguished. Moreover, our few noteworthy buildings are obscured by the dense development surrounding them.'

The plan recognised the changing requirements for more space and better facilities in the homes of tomorrow:

> The need for a larger kitchen is reinforced by modern standards of domestic equipment. The Dudley Report, for example, recommends two draining boards and a larger sink, storage cupboards and a working table-top. Refrigerators have become increasingly popular, and horizontal cookers take up about twice as much space as the vertical type. A wash boiler will also be required if laundering is to be done in the kitchen ... Alternatively a wash-house might be provided as an outbuilding.

They also recognised the social upheaval that large-scale redevelopment would cause, and wanted to put in its place something that would 'Induce a sense of local patriotism and an interest in community life.' Their plans were therefore built around neighbourhoods of about 10,000 people, each with their own community centre and facilities, which they see as the 'Modern urbanised version of the traditional village ... In due course, the neighbourhood centre will become the natural meeting-place for the local population; combined with the advantages which city life has to offer, it should enable the urban neighbourhood to reach a higher cultural level than is obtainable in the rural village.'

With typical confidence, they calculated how many square feet of shops each neighbourhood centre would need, even making allowance for future rises in the standard of living, though ideas such as the modern supermarket or the out-of-centre retail development were, of course, not on their radar. The idealism of their aspirations is in marked contrast to the critical things they had to say about their showpiece garden suburb of Wythenshawe:

> Like most large housing estates, it has a somewhat anae-mic social atmosphere – a lack of robust community life – attributable in part to its newness, but more particularly to the absence of good communal facilities. Responsible local residents have complained with justice of the lack of libraries, cinemas, dancehalls and other social necessities, of the inadequacy or inconvenience of the local shops and the medical services, and of the paucity of schools ...

It was one thing to plan all the facilities a community needs, but quite another to find the money and the political will to turn them into bricks and mortar. All of which brings us to the gulf between the plan's aspirations and the means of making them happen.

The minute detail of the plan's proposals was in marked contrast to the section dealing with how the plan would be turned into reality. The latter covered just over half a page of a 274-page document. The timetable was left vague, beyond saying the full scheme 'Was unlikely to approach ultimate completion in less than fifty years.' Where was the money to come from? 'It is, of course, assumed that adequate powers and financial facilities will be provided by the State, for otherwise no satisfactory scheme could possibly be put into effect.' And how much money would be needed? 'To forecast the total expenditure involved in carrying out the Plan would be virtually impossible, nor would such an estimate serve any useful purpose.'

REDEVELOPMENT IN REALITY

Until 1954, neither the city council nor the nation had the resources to do much more than repair bomb damage. By then, it was estimated that the city had some 70,000 homes unfit for human habitation, and the council set itself a target of clearing the first 7,500 of them over five years. At this rate, it would have taken almost half a century to remove the ones that were currently unfit, let alone those that became unfit in the mean time, but even this modest target was missed by 1,000. From 1960, they adopted a more ambitious programme, selecting Hulme, Beswick, Longsight and Harpurhey as the first areas for comprehensive redevelopment.

One big problem was deciding how to re-house populations living in impossibly high densities in the redevelopment areas. The council wisely ruled out high-rise flats, but their chosen solutions were by no means without problems. Deck access housing was rather like high-rise blocks laid on their side, with access to the flats being via what were optimistically called 'streets in the sky', which would be free from conflict between pedestrians and cars. About 3,000 of these dwellings were built in Hulme alone. In practice, the blocks generally turned out to be badly-designed, badly manufactured, badly assembled on site, not to mention badly-insulated, cold and damp. Naturally, they won architectural awards before they had to be pulled down.

Even with deck access, the council still could not put as many people back in the redeveloped areas as they displaced from the slums. So the other part of their solution was to find overspill sites outside the city boundaries. One of the problems with this was finding acceptable sites. Major schemes at Mobberley and Lymm were rejected by the government in the 1950s but, in the twenty years from 1953, almost 23,500 new homes were built in twenty-two locations. The largest developments were at Hattersley (near Hyde) and Langley (near Rochdale), each consisting of more than 4,000 homes. Common complaints about these were that they were too far away from sources of employment, that they lacked the facilities that made for proper communities, and that they helped to break up established communities in the redevelopment areas.

By the 1970s, the emphasis shifted away from wholesale clearance to refurbishing the best of the remaining older stock, with some 40,000 older houses being improved by the turn of the century. But this still left about a quarter of the city's housing stock in need of major renovation – much of it the houses that had been built in the 1960s and 1970s.

13

AND ANOTHER THING ...

In this section, we gather together some assorted snippets from the story of Manchester that did not fit into any of the other sections of the book.

THE START OF MANCHESTER

The earliest recorded settlement of Manchester, the first turf and timber Roman fort, was started in AD 79, the same year that Pompeii was buried by the eruption of Vesuvius. The first Mancunian whose name we know was a centurion called Massavo. He helped to build the first fort, and came from either western Germany or Holland. A.J.P. Taylor said of the remains of Manchester's Roman origins: 'It had a Roman foundation, though not worth lingering on. The fragment of a wall in a goods yard at the bottom of Deansgate ranks as the least interesting Roman remain in England, which is setting a high standard.'

MANCHESTER CASTLE

In addition to its Roman fort, Manchester once had a castle, which was built in Saxon times. However, it was described as being 'Of no political or military importance' and nobody even seems to be very sure today where it was – possibly on the site of what is today Chetham's School, where Robert Grelley, the thirteenth century Lord of the Manor, built his manor house.

MANCHESTER AND SALFORD

In the year 923, Manchester was simply one of the parishes forming the Royal Manor of Salford. However, by the eleventh century, St Mary's church in Manchester served as the mother church to the whole of the Salford Hundred (the Hundred was the medieval sub-division of the shire), making Manchester the ecclesiastical, if not the administrative, hub of the area. The two settlements fell into separate ownerships in about 1102, never to be reunited.

THE TEXTILE INDUSTRY

This appears to have been well-established in Manchester as early as the fourteenth century. There is a record of the town having a fulling mill (part of the textile-making process) in 1322. Some of the earliest 'Manchester cottons' were actually a form of woollen cloth.

UNUSUAL JOBS

The public authorities in Manchester have employed some people in strange posts over the years. They include:

Ale conners (or tasters) who made sure the local ale was of an acceptable quality, sold at regulated prices and in proper measures.

Winter watch – people who patrolled the streets between 10 p.m. and 5 a.m. on winter nights.

Preventers of the cutting and gashing of raw hides.

Town waits – a band of wind musicians, who had to parade as a marching band through the town and entertain at weddings and dinners.

Town swineherd who drove all the pigs out of the town in the morning and brought them all back at night.

Anti-sports development officer – no, he was not actually called that, but the job of this Elizabethan official was to stop people playing football in the streets. The Court Leet banned the practice in 1608, 1656 and 1657.

MANCHESTER GOES TO WAR

There was a general calling up of fighting men as Elizabethan England prepared to repel the Spanish Armada. Manchester was required to provide 38 gunners, 38 archers and 144 ordinary foot-soldiers – about half the total requirement for the whole of Lancashire.

MANCHESTER'S FIRST MP

As a reward for Manchester's support during the Civil War, Oliver Cromwell gave the town its first Member of Parliament. Colonel (later Major-General) Charles Worsley was elected by the town's burgesses. He lived in Platt Hall (in Platt Fields today) and it was to there that the parliamentary mace was taken, after Cromwell famously had it removed from the House of Commons. Worsley was at one time tipped as a possible successor to Cromwell, until his untimely death at the age of thirty-five, in 1656. One of Charles II's actions on his restoration to the throne was to strip Manchester of its MP. It would be 1838 before the town next had one.

MANCHESTER'S FIRST NEWSPAPER

This was not the *Guardian,* but the *Manchester Weekly Journal* of 1719. It contained no local news whatsoever and only survived until 1726. The *Manchester Mercury* was rather longer lived, being founded in 1752 and surviving until 1830, after the birth of the *Guardian.*

BLACKFRIARS BRIDGE

This was originally inspired by a group of comedians. They were appearing in Salford in 1761 and, in order to draw a greater audience from Manchester, they went to the lengths of constructing a wooden footbridge across the Irwell. They named it Blackfriars Bridge as an ironic reference to the much more substantial Blackfriars Bridge, then under construction across the Thames in London. The bridge proved to be a success (history does not record whether their comedy act was equally successful) and it was demolished in 1817 and later replaced by a more solid crossing.

THE FIRST RAILWAY TICKETS

The railway ticket was invented in 1837 by Thomas Edmondson, a clerk on the Manchester & Leeds Railway. Before then, passengers had to book in advance by filling in a form with their name, address, place of birth, age, occupation and reason for travelling (this information was to enable the railway company to inform next of kin, in the event of a disaster). Early tickets represented the destination by a symbol, since many of the ticket collectors would have been illiterate.

DEATHS ON THE RAILWAY

Early passengers on the Liverpool & Manchester Railway often failed to appreciate that railways were far faster (and therefore more dangerous) than horse-drawn transport. Among the early causes of death on the railway were: riding on the roof of the carriage and getting knocked off by the first bridge; leaping from a moving train to retrieve one's hat and falling asleep lying across the line.

FIVE LOCAL AUTHORITIES

Before 1838 Manchester was governed by no less than five separate authorities:

The Court Leet: A medieval survival, answerable to the Lord of the Manor, dealing with small debts and nuisances, and taking some of the responsibility for policing the town.

The Churchwardens and Overseers: They held the power to collect money for local services, and had both ecclesiastical and civic functions, the latter including the care of the poor, both inside and out of the workhouse.

The Police and Improvement Commissioners: They had responsibilities for the cleansing, lighting and watching of Manchester, as well as carrying out various improvements. They also supervised the night – but not the day – police.

The Surveyors of Highways: Who looked after local roads (except turnpikes, which had their own turnpike trusts).

The Justices of the Peace for the County: They had various duties, often overlapping with some of the above, and also ran the New Bailey Prison.

Between them, they collected six lots of rates:

The Poor Rate
The Police Rate
The Highway Rate
The County Rate
The Stipendiary Magistrate's Salary Rate
The Church Rate (no longer compulsory by 1838)

THREE POLICE FORCES!

In 1838, the town had three police forces, with no overall coordination:

The Day Police, under the control of the constables.

The Night Police, under the control of the Commissioners.

The Borough Police, under the control of Watch Committee of the Borough Council.

MANCHESTER AND THE IRISH

In 1835 the Poor Law Commissioners estimated that a fifth of Manchester's population was of Irish origin. The *Manchester Guardian* in 1829 described the Irish as 'The most serious social evil with which our labouring classes have to contend', and even Engels (who married an Irish woman) criticised them for their appalling living conditions and drunkenness.

DEATHS IN THE WORKHOUSE

The number of deaths recorded in the Manchester workhouse, from 1 September 1837 to 31 August 1838, were 295, the average number of inmates being 708. Thus, 1 out of every 2 and 8/20ths – or about 2½ – inmates died that year. However, it should be noted that 57 per cent of the inmates were listed as either 'Infirm and incapable of work or sick, and on the doctor's list'.

MANCHESTER UNITED'S LIVERPOOL CONNECTION

One of the 2,000 people employed at the railway works at Newton Heath was a superintendent engineer called Frederick Attock. He came from Liverpool and founded a football team from among the labour force. That team went on to become Manchester United – a team founded by a Scouser!

MANCHESTER'S COAT OF ARMS

Have you seen the city's coat of arms and wondered what it represented? You can always look it up at the official source and it will tell you:

> Gules, three bendlets enhanced Or; a chief argent, thereon on waves of the sea a ship under sail proper: On a wreath of colours, a terrestrial globe semee of bees Volant, all proper. On the dexter side a heraldic antelope argent. Attired, and chain reflexed over the back Or, and on the sinister side a lion guardant Or, morally crowned Gules; each charged on the shoulder with a rose of the last. Motto 'concilio et labore'.

All clear? I thought so. In English, it is a red shield with three diagonal gold stripes, a ship on the sea and a globe with flying bees on it, to represent Manchester's international trade and its claim to be the birthplace of the Industrial Revolution (the bees were adopted as a symbol of this claim in the nineteenth century). The antelope and chain represent the engineering industries, and the lion wears a crown in the shape of a castle, to remind us of Castlefield and the city's Roman origins. The roses the two beasts wear are the red rose of Lancashire and the motto means 'by wisdom and effort', or 'by counsel and hard work'.

LOST LANDMARKS

We have had a section on the landmark buildings that can still be seen – how about some of the ones we have lost?

The Oldest Pub?

The Seven Stars in Withy Grove used to claim to be the oldest licensed inn in Britain (though there are hostelries in other cities that dispute this claim). Its history went back to 1356. Tradition had it that the masons working on what became Manchester Cathedral used to pass their leisure there, and that Bonnie Prince Charlie billeted some of his troops in it in 1745. Its lease came up for renewal in 1911 and, as the *Manchester City News* of the day put it, 'The exigiencies of modern commerce demand its effacement'. Despite the efforts of early conservationists, it was demolished that same year.

St Peter's Church

This used to stand on what is now St Peter's Square, in front of the Central Library. It was a building in the Doric style, designed by the eminent architect James Wyatt (he also designed Heaton Hall) and was consecrated in 1794. It formed the backdrop to the events of the Peterloo Massacre. At first it had a very elite congregation; as one contemporary put it: 'There were no naughty people among them; most of them were rich and came to church in carriages.' However, these were precisely the type of people who would later join the flight to the suburbs. By the time of the 1901 census, only 390 people lived within its catchment, and it was closed in 1906.

Poets' Corner

Early photographs of Long Millgate show a romantically tumbledown group of seventeenth-century buildings, centred around the Sun Inn. This became known as Poets' Corner at the time when the licensee of the Sun was himself an amateur poet, and fellow enthusiasts used to assemble there for evenings of readings, ale, food and tobacco.

Assize Courts

'A magnificent pile in the decorated Gothic style' by Alfred Waterhouse. For most of those attending it (and particularly those doing so in the dock) it would be the grandest building they had ever entered. It opened for business in 1864, but was one of the victims of the Second World War bombing.

TEACHING THE LADIES

The education of women took a lesser priority with many of our forebears. Even the daughters of the well-heeled might expect only a limited education, in line with their limited opportunity to use it afterwards. In 1792, the *Manchester Mercury* announced that a Mrs Godfrey was opening a 'genteel Day School' for young ladies, where particular attention was to be paid to the art of reading and speaking with propriety.

If you enjoyed this book, you may also be interested in…

South Manchester Remembered

GRAHAM PHYTHIAN

Take a nostalgic journey into South Manchester's colourful past with this rich collection of tales from bygone days in Didsbury, Chorlton, Levenshulme, Rusholme, Northenden, and surrounding districts. Among the topics featured here are sporting events, marathons, ghosts, murders, and even buried treasure! Readable, informative and entertaining, this richly illustrated volume will intrigue and delight everyone who knows and loves the city of Manchester.

978 0 7524 7002 3

The Manchester Book of Days

BEN MCGARR

The Manchester Book of Days contains quirky, eccentric, shocking, amusing and important events and facts from different periods in the history of the city. Ideal for dipping into, this addictive little book will keep you entertained and informed. Featuring hundreds of snippets of information and covering the social, criminal, political, religious, agricultural, industrial and military history of the city, it will delight residents and visitors alike.

978 0 7524 8308 5

The Manchester Regiment:
The 63rd and 96th Regiments of Foot

ROBERT BONNER

This fascinating illustrated regimental history contains photographs between the 1860s and the last days of the Manchester Regiment in 1958, when it ceased to exist as a distinct unit. With 200 photographs from the Regiment's own archive at the Museum of the Manchester Regiment, many never before published, this volume provides an interesting pictorial insight into the history of the Regiment.

978 0 7524 6015 4